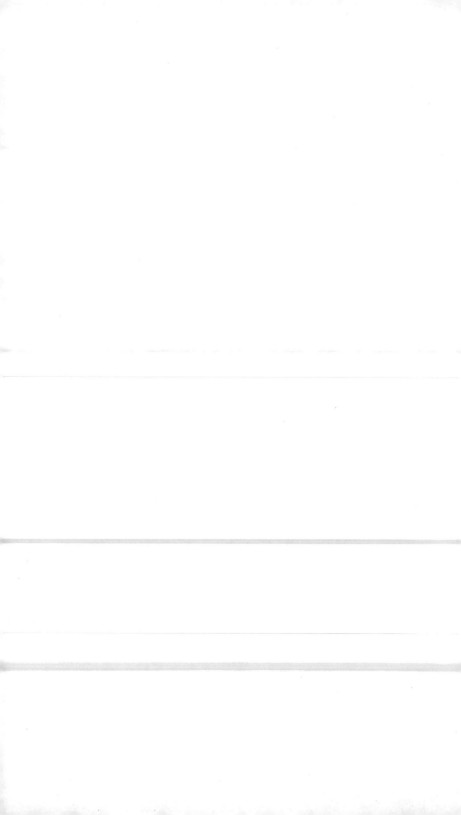

TWILIGHT OF A GREAT CIVILIZATION

TWILIGHT OF A GREAT CIVILIZATION

THE DRIFT TOWARD NEO-PAGANISM

Carl F. H. Henry

CROSSWAY BOOKS • WESTCHESTER, ILLINOIS
A DIVISION OF GOOD NEWS PUBLISHERS

First printing, 1988

Printed in the United States of America

Library of Congress Catalog Card Number 88-70393

ISBN 0-89107-491-0

———————

The publisher and author would like to express appreciation for permission to use the following materials:

"The Barbarians Are Coming," convocation address given at Eastern Baptist Theological Seminary in September 1969. Reprinted by permission from *Eternity* magazine, Vol. 20, No. 1, January 1970.

"Diagnosis of a Troubled Time," comments to the faculty of Asbury College on January 28, 1987, preliminary to a dialogue on the moral crisis of our times.

"Toward a Prescription for Recovery," comments to the faculty of Asbury College on January 28, 1987, preliminary to a dialogue on Christian social involvement.

"The Fight of the Day," a sermon preached at First Evangelical Free Church of Annandale, Virginia. This sermon also appears in *Best Sermons 1,* edited by James W. Cox and published by Harper & Row, San Francisco, 1988 and is included here by agreement with the editor.

"Beggars and Benefactors," a commencement address by Dr. Carl F. H. Henry, given at Calvin Theological Seminary, Grand Rapids, May 24, 1986.

"Are Theologians an Endangered Species?," a commencement address given at Westminster Theological Seminary, Philadelphia, on May 28, 1986.

"The Creator and the Neo-Pagan Mind," a message to the Pastors Conference of the Southern Baptist Convention in St. Louis, on June 15, 1987.

"Feed Them on Fantasies," reprinted by permission from *United Evangelical Action,* March-April 1986 issue, which titled these comments "Insights on Liberation Theology."

"Perspectives on Capital Punishment," remarks at the annual convention of the National Association of Evangelicals in Buffalo, New York, on March 5, 1987, in a Point/Counterpoint dialogue presided over by Dr. Daniel W. Van Ness, president of Justice Fellowship, and involving Dr. Myron Augsburger, adjunct professor of theology at Eastern Mennonite College, and Dr. Lynn R. Buzzard, professor of constitutional law at Campbell University School of Law.

"Where Will Evangelicals Cast Their Lot?," reprinted from *This World,* Summer 1987 issue.

"Facing the Crisis in Education," first appeared in *World,* Vol. 2, No. 25, February 22, 1988, under the title "Facing New Crises in Education."

"Educating for Intellectual Excellence," first appeared in abridged form in the March/April 1988 issue of *United Evangelical Action,* the official publication of the National Association of Evangelicals.

"Christian Fund-Raising Heresies." An edited version of this speech, given at a "Funding the Christian Challenge" conference in Kansas City, March 10, 1987, appears in *Funding the Evangelical Enterprise* (Victor Books, 1988).

"The Christian Worldview Imperative," used by permission from *Institute for Christian Leadership's Faculty Dialogue,* 1988.

"The Christian Scholar's Task in a Stricken World," first appeared in the June 1988 issue of *Christian Scholar's Review* (XVII: 4).

"The Judeo-Christian Heritage and Human Rights," copyright © 1986 Curators of the University of Missouri. Reprinted with permission. Originally delivered as a speech in September 1986 as part of the Paine Lectures on Religion.

"The Uneasy Conscience Revisited," address given on November 3, 1987, at the fortieth anniversary of the founding of Fuller Theological Seminary in Pasadena, California.

CONTENTS

PREFACE

---

*H*alf a generation ago, Dr. Carl F. H. Henry made an arresting claim: "The Barbarians Are Coming" and they threaten to undermine the foundations of Western civilization. To many in 1970 this must have seemed extreme; today, with the distintegration of morality and culture evident on every hand, it rings prophetically true.

The opening chapter of this book presents this original essay—with its penetrating assessment of our cultural malaise, its resounding affirmation of our Savior's ultimate victory, and its uncompromising call to proclaim and demonstrate the Good News of Jesus Christ in every area of culture. The succeeding chapters, all recent essays, explore these themes in relation to key areas where the church and the wider culture find themselves locked "in rival conflict for the mind, the conscience, the will, the spirit, the very selfhood of contemporary man."

The new barbarianism, Dr. Henry shows, grows out of a thoroughgoing humanistic rejection of God and the Judeo-Christian foundation of Western culture; but more than simply rejecting the legacy of the West, the new barbarianism has embraced a new pagan mentality. On one hand it proclaims that there is no fixed truth, no final good, no ultimate meaning and purpose, and that the living God is a primitive illusion. On the other hand, it champions mysticism, occult forces and powers, communion with nature, and exotic religions. And where these pagan impulses hold sway the results are moral and intellectual decay paralleled only by Pompeii and Sodom—not to mention the bloody American abortion of twenty million unborn children.

Do we as Christians clearly see and understand the tragic drift of our culture? Has not the secular world sometimes been more aware of the crisis than we have? Thus Allan Bloom writes that "higher education has failed democracy and impoverished the souls of today's students." *Time* does a cover story on "ethics" which asks penetrating questions and wonders how we might recover our moral bearings, but provides few answers. And *Newsweek* concludes in a special report on the decline of America: "The American Century is over; the world order is changing. But America's eclipse is not inevitable. In a country where people can choose..., the future... is a matter of choice."

What we choose has decisive and perhaps irrevocable significance. As Moses proclaimed to ancient Israel:

> This day I call heaven and earth as witnesses against you that I have set before you life and death, blessings and curses. *Now choose life,* so that you and your children may live and that you may love the Lord your God, listen to his voice, and hold fast to him. For the Lord is your life... (Deut. 30:19, 20a, emphasis added)

The choice we face, just as did ancient Israel, is between the living God and the pagan gods of our age; between light and darkness; between life and death. It impinges on business and on the home, on education and on the arts, on our private lives and on the wider culture. In confronting this question Dr. Henry's insights, shared in the following pages, will prove an invaluable resource to all who long for the light of Christ to shine with brilliance in this "the twilight of a great civilization."

—*Lane T. Dennis, Ph.D.*
President, CROSSWAY BOOKS

PART ONE:

THE RISE OF NEO-PAGANISM

THE BARBARIANS
ARE COMING

W e live in the twilight of a great civilization, amid the deepening decline of modern culture. Those strange beast-empires of the books of Daniel and Revelation seem already to be stalking and sprawling over the surface of the earth. Only the experimental success of modern science hides from us the dread terminal illness of our increasingly technological civilization.

Because our sights are fixed on outer space and man on the moon, we cannot see the judgment that hangs low over our own planet. We applaud modern man's capability but forget that nations are threatening each other with atomic destruction, that gunsmoke darkens our inner cities, and that our near-neighbors walk in terror by day and sleep in fear by night. We sit glued to television sets, unmindful that ancient pagan rulers staged Colosseum circuses to switch the minds of the restless ones from the realities of a spiritually-vagrant empire to the illusion that all is basically well.

We are so steeped in the antichrist philosophy—namely, that success consists in embracing not the values of the Sermon on the Mount but an infinity of material things, of sex and status—that we little sense how much of what passes for practical Christianity is really an apostate compromise with the spirit of the age.

Our generation is lost to the truth of God, to the reality of divine revelation, to the content of God's will, to the power of His redemption, and to the authority of His Word. For this loss it is paying dearly in a swift relapse to paganism. The savages are stirring again; you can hear them rumbling and rustling in the tempo of our times.

1. *The barbarians are coming.* All our scientific achievement can be misused by those coming barbarians for their cruel and cunning deeds. Hitler and the Nazis have already deployed twentieth-century scientific know-how to cremate people by the hundreds of thousands in those highly efficient gas chambers. Stalin and other totalitarian tyrants long ago learned that captive mass media could enslave myriads of modern men. Red Chinese warlords seem eager to play with atomic fire, although the bombs that fell on Hiroshima and Nagasaki are now but mini-versions of our maxi-weapons.

Year by year the probability of a globally-destructive nuclear war increases; the Nobel prizeman George Wald, a leading renowned biologist, speaking at M.I.T., said that a distinguished professor of government at Harvard calculates the accelerating odds for a full-scale nuclear war to be one chance in three by 1990, one chance in two by the year 2000. All our scientific know-how can be deployed for destructive ends.

2. *The barbarians are coming.* Reason and persuasion are giving way to mob pressure and revolution as the approved means of social change. Anyone can play this game of compulsion if he has enough social dynamite. But the price is another nail in the coffin of democratic processes. Down the road are the approaching caravans of the Machiavellis and Leviathans and those might-makes-right despots.

Colleges and universities are faltering as the intellectually critical centers of society; some have even become launch-pads for social anarchy. The confusion and chaos of society have moved onto the campuses and into the classrooms of our schools; in the name of democratic pluralism major educational institutions forsake the name of God, pride themselves on academic excellence while they neglect objective truth, disagree on ultimate values, and bend to the anti-intellectualistic temper of our times.

In *Enemies of the Permanent Things* Russell Kirk puts the modern predicament this way: "The fountains of the great deep seem to be broken up in our time. Institutions that have endured for a millennium are awash, and the surly question before us, is whether the whole fabric of civilization can survive the present rate of economic and social alteration."

3. *The barbarians are coming.* Institutional Christianity has dropped the last barricade to the return of the pagan man; preoccupied with the changing of social structures, it muffles the call

for a new humanity, and in doing so forfeits a mighty spiritual opportunity at the crossroads of modern history. The organized Church that ought to have been burdened for the evangelization of the earth has been too busy either powdering her nose to preserve an attractive public image, or powdering the revolutionaries and reactionaries who need rather to be remade in Christ's image.

Disillusionment over organized Christianity is soaring; one can see it in the statistics of declining church attendance and of diminishing denominational giving, and in second thoughts about the ecumenical projection of one great world-church. While ecumenists stress that the strides toward church union commend Christ to the world, a whole generation is growing up with no awareness of regeneration by the Holy Spirit, a species without clear ideas about sin and sacrilege, a race for whom God and the supernatural are virtually eclipsed, individuals with no interest in the *imago Dei,* no eternal concerns.

The forerunners of these half-men are being nourished wherever a pulpit no longer preaches the commandments of God and the sinfulness of man, the ideal humanity of Jesus Christ and the divine forgiveness of sins, and the fact of saving grace. Obscure the vitalities of revealed religion, detour churchgoers from piety and saintliness, and in the so-called enlightened nations not only will the multitudes soon relapse to a retrograde morality, but churchgoers will live in Corinthian immorality, churchmen will encourage situational ethics, and the line between the Christian and the worldling will scarce be found. Even in the church barbarians are breeding: beware, the Scripture says, of the lawless one who will occupy the temple of God (2 Thess. 2:4). Savages are stirring the dust of a decadent civilization and already slink in the shadows of a disabled Church.

Those coming barbarians do not have the future to themselves, however. *Jesus Christ the Lord is coming:* we know it not simply by a whisper in the wind, we know it by His Word. He came once; He comes again.

1. *Jesus Christ the Lord is coming:* the Lord of Truth, to overwhelm all doubts. What hiding place then, when the-God-who-is-there, rewarder of all that diligently seek Him, acts to judge the secrets of men (Rom. 2:15)? What hiding place then for

the big lie that dialectical materialism fully explains the whole of reality, for those who say the supernatural is but a myth? What hiding place then for God-is-dead buffoons, when the living God who declares man to be dead in trespasses and sins calls these dead to judgment? What hiding place then for God-may-be-alive theorists, when the self-revealing God asks what men have done with the truth of revelation? What hiding place then for God-is-only-love religionists, when the Lord who desires truth in the inward parts asks whether men have obeyed the truth? Jesus Christ, the Lord of Truth, is coming: we know it by His Word.

2. *Jesus Christ the Lord is coming*: the King of kings to overpower all reluctant powers. What hiding place then for totalitarian tyrants when "at the name of Jesus every knee shall bow... and every tongue confess that Jesus Christ is Lord" (Phil. 2:11)? What hiding place then for the nations East or West who trust in atomic stockpiles? What hiding place then for Israel or Arab powers spilling their blood for holy land and holy city while the Holy One of Israel still hangs crucified outside the gates? What hiding place then for heathen nations still mired in darkness, and for Gentile nations whose scorn of God is scandal to the pagan world? Jesus Christ, the King of kings, is coming: we know it by His Word.

3. *Jesus Christ the Lord is coming*: the Man of Righteousness, to overflow the grace of God, but to override all scorners. He returns and overturns: in the final resurrection of the dead He overturns the whole human race: those who reject Him He turns to rout and everlasting separation; those who love Him He turns fully into the holy image of God. He comes to vindicate the righteousness of God and to crown the grace of God. Jesus Christ, the Lord of life and Lord of all, is coming—of creation life, of redemption life, of resurrection life. Jesus Christ our Lord is coming; we know it by His Word.

The barbarians are coming; the Lord Jesus Christ is coming: *Christians are here now: do they know whether they are coming or going?*

To the world we seem like Hogan's Army waiting for Godot. Can we take a holy initiative in history? Can we once more strike an apostolic stride? Can we put an ungodly world on the defensive again? Can we show men the folly of opposing Him who has already overcome the world, of rejecting fellowship with the coming King? Will we offer civilization a realistic option, or only a warning of impending doom? Will Christianity speak only to man's fears and frustrations, or will it also fill the vacuums in his heart and crown his longings for life at its best?

Unless evangelical Christians break out of their cultural isolation, unless we find new momentum in the modern world, we may just find ourselves so much on the margin of the mainstream movements of modern history that soon ours will be virtually a Dead Sea Caves community. Our supposed spiritual vitalities will be known only to ourselves, and publicly we will be laughed at as a quaint but obsolescent remnant from the past.

Institutional Christianity is already in very deep trouble. Liberal theology has only a political importance now, and even here its marriage to the god of revolution begets no criterion for distinguishing the divine from the demonic. Future historians may well look back upon our own lifetime as that very point in church history when the Christian churches forfeited their greatest spiritual opportunity since the apostolic age by making a fetish of church union, devoting millions upon millions of dollars to ecclesiastical administration and buildings, sounding an unclear gospel from a blurred Bible, debating the task of Christianity in the world on the mass media, and all the while losing evangelistic momentum.

The Christian Church is here with a global mandate and a great commission. Will the multitudes in the streets hear a stirring in the wind and sense afresh that Pentecost is blowing our way? Will they recognize that a new option does remain for them?

1. *The Church of Jesus Christ is here.* We must march and sing our faith again in the public arena—in the streets and on the mass media—not hide our light under church buildings and inside seminary walls. It was in the open marketplace that the Apostle Paul engaged Stoic and Epicurean philosophers in debate.

God's commandments need once again to become an issue in national life, the truth of revelation a matter of contention in every sphere of modern culture, the call for social righteousness a cause of trembling in every vale of injustice and indecency in the land. Neither modern scientists nor modern historians stand a ghost of a chance of burying and bolting Jesus of Nazareth in a Palestinian tomb unless we shroud Him through our silence, unless we keep quiet about the way God acts and speaks and about the sure future toward which He is guiding all history.

The Church often tells the world where it is going; does the Church today any longer know where she is going? The Church of Jesus Christ is here and has her marching orders: our mandate is His Word. Everything else around us is on the move: have we opted out of the contest for the mind and will and heart of modern man?

BREAKING DOWN FENCES

2. *The Church of Jesus Christ is here*—not white or black, not West or East, not denominational or nondenominational, but transracial, transnational, transdenominational. Breaking down our fences we must link hands and hearts with Christian believers of every race and region in a mutual thrust for evangelical faith in evangelism, education, and social involvement. If while evangelizing we abandon education to alien philosophies, we shall abet a climate that condemns Christianity as a religion for anti-intellectuals only. We shall veil the fact that the reasons given for modern unbelief are invalid rationalizations. We shall obscure the truth that evangelical theism involves a compelling intellectual commitment.

If while evangelizing we abandon the sociopolitical realm to its own devices, we shall fortify the misimpression that the public order falls wholly outside the command and will of God, that Christianity deals with private concerns only; and we shall conceal the fact that government exists by God's will as His servant for the sake of justice and order. Wherever man's distress threatens his humanity the Church of Christ has something desperately relevant to say, and is wholly obligated to say it. Be silent about it, and even some pagans will respond as Christians ought to, while others will exploit the valleys of discontent for political advantage or for their own personal benefit.

But if we seek to capture men's minds, and struggle for just social structures, yet neglect the evangelization of the earth, we shall fail our generation where it needs help most of all. Walter Lippmann has ventured to answer his own question "whether anything can be done soon enough to cope with the problems before they engulf us," by saying: "It isn't that it's beyond human nature's capacity to do it; it's that human nature is so lazy and selfish and often corrupt that it doesn't do it." As Malcolm Muggeridge once put it: "the most extraordinary thing about human beings" is the fact "that they pursue ends which they know to be disastrous and turn their backs on ways which they know to be joyous." Do we not see that what's wrong with modern man is precisely what the apostolic church diagnosed as the root of the problem of fallen man everywhere: a sinful heart that does not love God and neighbor? No stocking the mind, no altering the environment, will fully work the change that God demands: "Ye must be born again. . . . Except a man be born again he cannot see the Kingdom of God" (John 3:7, 3).

The Church of Jesus Christ is here, mandated with a mission personal and public, a mission transdenominational, transnational, transcultural: our mandate is His Word.

3. *The Church of Jesus Christ is here:* in a world halting between pseudo-lords and the Lord of lords, here with a specific message to proclaim, not merely a mission of projects and methods to probe. She is entrusted with God's truth, not with man-made theories: our mandate is His Word. The late twentieth century is bone-weary of the indefinite and inconclusive and indecisive; what it needs is a sure Word of God. A Church that forsakes the truth of revelation soon yields to the detouring modernity of the youngsters or to the crippling tradition of the elders, and will "teach as doctrines the commandments of men" (Mark 7:8).

The coming barbarians have no real future; neither has a Church that forsakes the truth of God. The Word of God is given, incarnate and incomparable, inscripturate and indelible. That God has revealed Himself intelligibly; that Jesus of Nazareth is the incarnate Logos of God; that the Scriptures are the Word of God written; that the Holy Spirit uses the truth of God as the means of human persuasion and conviction; that not even the twentieth century can cancel God's truth; not that the Word of God is bound but that all who neglect it are in a tragic bind—these emphases our generation needs desperately to hear.

"Thus saith the Lord!" is the only barricade that can save our unheeding generation from inevitable calamity. When all is said and tried, modern man's alternatives are either a return to the truth of revelation, even to the Bible as the unpolluted reservoir of the will of God, or an ever deeper plunge into meaninglessness and loss of worth.

In the twilight traffic snarl of a great civilization, the Church needs as never before to be a light to the world and to shelter the moral fortunes of human history from crippling collision. To hold the road for Jesus Christ requires authoritative charting, clarity of vision, and divine enabling. The Church is here at the crossroads. Open the Bible again: our mandate is His Word. The Church is here—called to a living exposition of the truth of revelation.

The barbarians are coming; the Lord Jesus Christ is coming; let the Church that is here come *now*, with good news, with the only durable good news, and come in time!

DIAGNOSIS OF A TROUBLED TIME

A half-generation ago when, after a span of editorial work, I returned to seminary teaching, I remarked in 1970 at a public convocation in Philadelphia that barbarians had already begun to invade the beleaguered civilization of the West, and that the Christian vanguard has two significant responses. Jesus Christ is coming and, I said, He will have the final word about history and is in fact even now judging the barbarians and us. But no less important than the coming of the barbarians and than the coming of the risen Jesus, I stressed, is the fact that Christ's regenerate Church is here on earth now with a definitive message and dynamic to hold the barbarians at bay.

I

That was a half-generation ago. What has now changed is that both the pagan forces and the Christian forces have accelerated their initiative and seem increasingly locked into a life-and-death struggle.

Paganism is now more deeply entrenched than in the recent past, and it holds a firmer grip on Western society. Given the present historical dynamisms, my view is that in another half-generation—before the turn of the century—humanism will have lost its humanism and the regenerate Church will survive in the social context of naked naturalism and raw paganism. The Christian Church—or some significant remnant of it—may indeed experience renewal, and it may even achieve spectacular gains on Mainland China and in certain African and Asian Third World countries. But that is another story, one marginal to the moral destiny of the West and to the fate of American evangelicalism.

I rule out for the present the dread possibility of nuclear war, not because human beings are too moral to risk it, nor because Star Wars can assuredly frustrate it, but because the human instinct for self-survival may preclude it. Yet Herbert Butterfield was assuredly right when he observed that it is consistent with the character of God that He might allow civilization to destroy itself by the very means that it idolatrously trusts for its security. Although I believe in the need for a strong defense in an age of predatory powers, it wrenches my spirit to know that in the horrendously expensive arms race to which the great powers are currently committed the price of just a single missile could establish a Christian university, even if that missile might need to be in place to preserve our religious freedom to establish it. Yet the final fate of our planet will be determined by God who made and sustains it. Modern political theory is riddled with practical atheism, since it dismisses God as irrelevant to the peace and perpetuity and prosperity of the nations.

The naturalistic thesis, that God has only subjective significance and counts for nothing in the ordering of nature and history, and is unrelated to the definition of truth and the distinction of right and wrong, prevails not only in the Communist world but today has a decisive grip on many intellectuals in the so-called Free World. Yet not even the right of political self-determination, on which the democracies so vigorously insist, is self-evident; it presupposes objective rights grounded in a transcendent moral order that secular political scientists blur. The entire corpus of human rights is today in peril, because none of the divergent contemporary philosophical theories can sustain fixed and universal rights; yet secular juridical scholars hesitate to return to a Judeo-Christian grounding for rights. That reluctance to reaffirm a Biblical, theistic framework for human rights and duties prevails even though no other view convincingly refutes the Marxist theory that the state alone has the prerogative of sovereignly stipulating all human rights.

A half-generation ago Free World spokesmen already had abandoned any prospect of fomenting and supporting a counter-revolution internal to Soviet-sphere countries, although they still spoke of the Communist world's imminent collapse under the weight of its own weaknesses. But in 1967, the militantly atheistic cultural revolution overtook Mainland China, controlling one-fourth of the world's population and much of its landmass. Today the intellectual weaknesses in the Marxist scheme are usually summarized in terms of repressive totalitarian bureaucracy and Socialist economics, which continues to fascinate Third World countries even though it is almost everywhere in difficulty. The Free World pressure for religious liberty in Eastern Europe is seldom correlated with the indispensable priority of God for a truly meaningful human life.

The startling spread of secular theory continues as a major phenomenon of the twentieth century. No Christian statesman foresaw in 1900 that our era would be marked by a massive defection, unparalleled in history, by descendants of Christian parents; instead, evangelicals spoke of winning the world for Christ in a single generation. From a mere 0.2 percent of the world population in 1900, atheists grew in number to 20.8 percent in 1980; increasing by 8.5 million a year, atheists by 1984 totalled one billion, a number that includes liberal humanists and skeptical nonbelievers as well as dialectical materialists. More rather than less countries than in 1970 are now officially atheistic; in fact, during the last fifteen years atheism added sixty million adherents.

The so-called Christian West was the context in which this secular tide gained early momentum. During the past half-generation secular humanism has widened its influence in America through the mass media, public education, and political theory. Despite mobilization of the fundamentalist-evangelical right by Moral Majority, that heavily-financed movement achieved not a single piece of desired legislation, and the changing political scene may soon revert the public influence of the religious right to the 1980 level.

The tendency to treat human beings as so much "live meat" to be held hostage or to sacrifice on the altar of personal convenience or monetary gain is widespread. A half-generation ago even some of the largest Protestant denominations in America already approved abortion-on-demand, and many Catholics practiced it. Despite the vigorous condemnation by protest groups, Americans now destroy a million-and-a-half unborn children a year; during the past decade abortions in the United States are thought to have exceeded ten million. The ancient pagan world widely practiced infanticide either for economic reasons or to control the number of births; Paul Ramsey suggests that modern abortion is a matter of "feticide."

The proliferation of terrorism—including the skyjacking of international flights—mirrors a growing readiness to barter human life for political ends. Terrorism is no longer the senseless behavior of a few mindless individuals; it is a carefully planned form of political violence that deliberately rejects civilizational norms and values. Since the killing of eleven Israeli Olympic athletes in 1972 in Munich, terrorism has accelerated to include the kidnapping of innocent victims, who are tortured by isolation and separation from kin, and held for ransom or murdered. Such crimes flout all the laws of civilized behavior; moreover, the Muslim Allah is held to be glorified by Shiite reliance on violence to extend Koranic power.

Another evidence of the deepening secular inroad is the shifting pattern of sexual behavior. This is manifest in the increasing rejection of monogamous marriage, the ready accommodation of divorce and its penetration into the church community and even into the marital commitment of the clergy, the legitimation of homosexuality and of lesbianism as alternative lifestyles. In the United States a million teenagers become pregnant annually despite sex education. The rapid acceleration of AIDS—Surgeon General C. Everett Koop says it may become history's deadliest epidemic which, unchecked, could kill one hundred million people worldwide by the year 2000—has served recently as a deterrent to sexual promiscuity. More than a million Americans are held to be already infected. But the public argument shifts the emphasis to undesirable consequences instead of focusing on the root cause: sexual promiscuity and the lack of monogamous relationships. Television and the print media pander to the lower emotions and make erotic relationships dramatically attractive. So indecent have the sex flicks become that even the U.S. Attorney General's office now regards as tame some magazines which as recently as a decade ago were considered patently pornographic. If ancient Pompeii was a world center for kinky sex, the media more and more channel eroticism into the homes of viewers. They have played a major role in making sports a national religion, in promoting the consumption of alcoholic beverages despite the national vice of alcoholism, and in publicizing lotteries that encourage the masses to gamble away their hard-won earnings.

These factors—the extensive loss of God through a commanding spread of atheism, the collapse of modern philosophical supports for human rights, the brutish dehumanization of life which beyond abortion and terrorism could encourage also a future acceptance even of nuclear war, and a striking shift of sexual behavior that welcomes not only divorce and infidelity but devious alternatives to monogamous marriage as well—attest that radical secularism grips the life of Western man more firmly than at any time since the pre-Christian pagan era.

Still more disconcerting is the fact that modernity deliberately experiences this new immorality as an option superior to the inherited Judeo-Christian alternative. What underlies the atheistic commitment to novel sexual and marital and political patterns is a stultification of Biblical conscience, an irreligious redefinition of the good, a profane willset. Modern mankind has forfeited self-understanding in relationship to the supernatural Creator and the salvific Christ. A half-generation ago the pagans were still largely threatening at the gates of Western culture; now the barbarians are plunging into the oriental and occidental mainstream. As they seek to reverse the inherited intellectual and moral heritage of the Bible, the Christian world-life view and the secular world-life view engage as never before in rival conflict for the mind, the conscience, the will, the spirit, the very selfhood of contemporary man. Not since the apostolic age has the Christian vanguard faced so formidable a foe in its claims for the created rationality and morality of mankind. The ancient speculation against which Christianity first contended, moreover, not only conceded but even insisted on what is now in deep dispute: the existence of supranatural divinity, the supra-animality of human beings, and the fixed objectivity of truth and the good.

II

So demanding and so complicated and confused is the conflict over morality and immorality today that everyone is prone to wonder at times whether all the choices we make may not really reduce to personal preferences after all. We all choose to do what we choose to do, of course, but the larger question is whether any transcendent ought confronts our moral choices.

Christianity says that human beings are inescapably answer-

27

able to a transcendent, objective good. God has personally revealed Himself and moreover, Christianity affirms, in doing so He has conveyed articulate moral principles and commandments—in short, a divine-command morality that stipulates how we ought to live. The written revelation of God, the Bible, is the sourcebook and standard of Christian morality.

Not only do atheists complicate the current ethical debate, but non-Christian theists and other speculative philosophers do so also, and Christians themselves often do not much help their own cause.

The very definition of justice is up for grabs today as it has not been since New Testament times. For starters, there is Biblical justice, Communist justice, modern liberal Western justice (which the Khomeini regime denounces as tolerant of sexual permissiveness and other vices), Shiite justice (which many Iranian revolutionaries who helped to enthrone it must now wish they could escape), and Islamic justice generally. Islam is theistic and yet, not much differently than atheistic communism, although in the name of Allah, it can justify terrorism and wield the sword to extend Koranic influence; moreover, in a supreme suppression of religious liberty, it approves beheading a Muslim who forsakes his faith.

No less confusing is the fact that the modern struts for morality are conflicting and inconclusive. The appeal is sometimes made to tradition (of which there are a variety), human welfare (Augustine and Marx and Hitler differ greatly about what this requires), utilitarianism (although the "greatest good of the greatest number" leaps roughshod over minorities), evolutionary progress (as if this somehow reached its apex in the present generation), and even natural law. Modern natural law theories are humanistic to the core and delete God as a referent; even those which insist more traditionally on a universal Creator (as Thomas Aquinas did) do not wholly agree on the content of natural law.

TOWARD A PRESCRIPTION FOR RECOVERY

Given the complexity of modern life, can Christians who affirm a Biblically-grounded morality really bridge from ancient Scripture to pressing contemporary ethical dilemmas such as the uses of nuclear power, abortion, surrogate motherhood, and much else? In a time of rampant ethical diversity, what Christian countermoves are appropriate in promoting morally-preferred legislation? Are all the Scriptural imperatives to be brought forward into contemporary life and, if not, on what basis do Christians distinguish the permanent from the temporary? On what ground do Christians ideally promote Biblically-acceptable options in a democratic society that champions separation of church and state? My comments aim to shed light on these concerns.

1. Don't think God has ordained you to carry the entire space-time universe on your own back. God created it, God sustains it, and God intends that "the government will be upon his [Messiah's] shoulder" (Isa. 9:6). In this life we humans are neither infallible nor impeccable, however much we try. Thank God for the forgiveness of sins, for the new birth and a place in His Kingdom, for the substituted Savior who alone is "the Just and Holy One."

2. This necessary reminder, however, doesn't get you and me off the hook morally. God wishes to win through our trust and obedience the same dramatic victory over world-evil and temptation that He did through His beloved Son. Jews who complain that Christians are more interested in faith than in justice or righteousness may describe some churchgoers, but they are wrong in principle. True faith and righteousness/justice are two sides of one and the same coin. If we call only for justice, we will all end up in hell, since "the wages of sin is death." If we call only for

"faith" (without works—faith that the New Testament calls "dead"), we will end up with neither true faith nor justice and face the same destiny. Authentic faith and a commitment to righteousness/justice go hand in glove.

3. What then shall we do? Inspired Scripture, writes Paul, equips believers "for good work of every kind" (2 Tim. 3:17). The place to begin, therefore, is to do in good conscience what the Bible expressly enjoins us to do, to strive to embrace God with all our being and our neighbor as ourselves, to welcome the fullness of the Holy Spirit, to follow Jesus' example of moral obedience, to keep the commandments of God, to emulate the holy and just One by living out the will of God.

4. To be sure, not all Old Testament ethics is meant for today. The Hebrew theocracy is gone, along with the laws that were reserved for it, including the death penalty for adultery, for incest, for sodomy, for perjury, for witchcraft, for abusing parents, for blasphemy, for Sabbath-breaking, for false teaching, for sacrificing to false gods. Capital punishment for murder, on the other hand, has a pre-theocratic status. We are to follow the lead of the New Testament in what is carried forward from the Old. Jesus Christ fulfills the ceremonial law and annuls it; He fulfills the moral law and perpetuates it. To deserve approval by civil authorities, Paul writes the Christians in Rome, they are to "do right" (Rom. 13:4), and he then puts the social commandments of the law (against killing, stealing and coveting) on the agenda of public righteousness and makes them a test of neighbor-love. The Mosaic commandments reappear in the book of Revelation in the comprehensive context of the final judgment of men and nations; they have enduring importance.

5. The Christian life is life in the Holy Spirit, not life governed by detailed regulations as was the life of God's people in Old Testament times. The New Testament does contain a few rules (e.g., "Pay just wages"; "pay your taxes"), but the believer under the authority of Scripture is spiritually liberated to keep the moral law in good conscience in a diversity of cultural contexts and political structures. The risen Lord rules the regenerate Church by the Holy Spirit through the Scriptural Word.

6. On many important contemporary issues we are left to make inferences from such Biblically-revealed principles as the dignity of human life, the corruption of human nature, the indispensable role of civil government. The Bible does not directly

settle what these principles imply for some crucial social concerns. Shall we, for example, rely on nuclear energy even for peaceful purposes, rather than on more traditional alternatives, despite menacing reactor malfunction possibilities and waste disposal problems? On such issues Christians have no more knowledge than do humanists or other non-Christians who weigh the probabilities for harm against the probabilities for good. To be sure, Christians will decide the matter not on the basis only of economic factors, or of selfish advantage to the present generation, but in view of the value of human life and of ecological concerns alongside constructive harnessing of the forces of nature. But one nonetheless makes the best decision he can in view of the available empirical data illuminated by biblical principles. Logical implications and inference yield valid doctrine, as in the case of the doctrine of the Trinity. But not all inferences we venture to draw from Scripture are infallible.

7. Church tradition serves to indicate what ecclesiastical scholars have previously inferred from Scripture, but such tradition is not infallible. Only the so-called apostolic tradition, Scripture as a literary corpus, is divinely inspired and authoritative. The debate over nuclear war attests that believers can and do reach rival conclusions on major social concerns. Some Christians consider war the worst of all evils; nuclear or non-nuclear, they regard war as essentially in violation of Jesus' command of neighbor-love. Others, in view of Paul's teaching on civil government (Rom. 13:4), hold that predatory acts by aggressor nations ought to be resisted and contained, lest more assertive behavior be encouraged. Some consider nuclear missiles so potentially destructive of human life and the cosmos that they would ban them completely; others hold that only the counter-threat of nuclear response can effectively challenge the will of contemporary predator powers. All agree that war is a catastrophic evil; they differ over whether it is the worst of all national evils, or whether physical nonresistance that leads to the loss of liberty outstrips it. Such crucial moral choices involve the risk of being wrong. Whatever stand we take, we need sufficient reason and good conscience, and we must stand ready to suffer the consequences of the positions we hold.

8. Christianity does not exist to guarantee felicitous survival to a world that insists upon rejecting God as the supreme source of its security. The Church is to be light, salt and leaven to the world, but it is not nor can it be salt that forever preserves a world

indifferent to the light. The Church is light, leaven, and salt on two frontiers, one evangelistic and the other political. She is under mandate to preach the gospel to all the world and to make disciples of all nations. If she fails to do so, not only is the world's doom sealed, but the survival of the Church is also imperiled.

The Church is not only to proclaim the gospel at the edges of history, but she is to exemplify the standards by which at the end of history Christ will judge the world and is in fact already even now judging it. She is to herald the availability of salvation for all who repent and receive and follow Christ. The Church must leave no doubt that she serves a supernatural, self-revealing God, and that she is entrusted with the very Word and will of God, proclaims divinely revealed truths and commands, and offers a divinely vouchsafed redemption. To perceive the Church only in terms of ethical and salvific probabilities, and not as the bearer of moral absolutes and soteric imperatives, is to eclipse her transcendent Ground. Our message to contemporary paganism is not that murder is wrong except when Jews are involved, or that there is an 89 percent probability that Jesus Christ died for our sins. It is that God's image in mankind is deposed whenever one murders a fellow human being, and that "there is no other name under heaven whereby we must be saved." That God speaks, God commands, God promises, God threatens, God invites—that is the Church's evangelistic message to the world. The Church must proclaim that message from the pulpit and through the media not merely to the people of God, but especially to worldlings who remain living prospects for redemptive rescue and renewal.

9. Just as the state is not to exploit the Church for political purposes, so the Church is not to use political mechanisms to force beliefs and practices upon society at large. As citizens of two worlds, Christians are indeed obliged to participate in political affairs to the limit of their ability and competence; the price of withdrawal is to be ruled by nonbelievers and to forfeit the vocational leadership and service of believers. Since legislation is concerned with human behavior, almost all laws have moral implications. Christians have no less right than other citizens to reflect their views into the public arena, and to give public reasons why some legal options are better than others. In political discourse, however, Christians will preferably use the rhetoric of a republic or the dialogue of a democracy. That is, Christians will not routinely press their political views on the ground of special revela-

tion; were they to do so, Mormons, Muslims and others would quickly do the same. The state is not the ultimate judge of metaphysical alternatives, a prerogative that totalitarian powers assume. In the public arena it is necessary to appeal to public reason. The Christian can effectively employ *ad hominum* argument and show that even on the secular world's premises—whether it appeals to tradition, to majority opinion, to common welfare, or to utility—the world cannot show that the options Christians champion are inferior to projected secular alternatives.

Negatively there are many traditions; positively, the Christian tradition has more to commend it than do the alternatives. Negatively, majority opinion can be and often is wrong, and conscience needs corrective guidance; positively, a moral majority can be the social conscience of a nation. Negatively, human welfare is competitively defined by Augustine, Hitler, Marx and others; positively, social justice best guarantees the welfare of society. Negatively, the greatest good of the greatest number often neglects the rights of minorities; positively, public righteousness promotes the greatest good for all. These arguments do not ground Christian options in world-speculative moral notions, all of which today are in collapse. Rather, they emphasize that secular alternatives are inferior to a preferable option. Yet it is important to remember that politics is not a mechanism for bringing in the Kingdom of God; positive law reaches for approximations of the ideal, but it nonetheless is vulnerable to continuing revision and refinement.

10. The Christian knows that all human beings participate in general or universal divine revelation. Proponents of traditional natural law theory exaggerate the consequences by holding that mankind everywhere shares an agreed body of ethical doctrine. Such natural law theory, in my view, is too optimistic about the perverse role of the will in fallen human experience, and it appeals to special revelation too late in the argument to preserve its significance. Yet on the basis of the *imago Dei* that universally survives the Fall, even if blurred, the Christian can declare even of the nonbeliever that concerning certain moral emphases, "in your heart you know it's right." Even though natural law theory overstates its content in terms of a universally shared system of morality, some remnants of a creation-ethic survive in the conscience of every human being. These include not only formal aspects of the *imago Dei* but a specific content, although that content does not constitute a universally shared body of ethical doctrine.

11. The appeal to public reason in political disputation does not preclude the Church from affirming on appropriate occasions that its moral absolutes derive from special divine revelation. Such occasions arise when civil government requires Christians to act contrary to the revealed will of God; when the Church is requested to testify to its position on specific issues in legislative committee hearings; and when the Church as Church sets itself against intractable injustice in the sociopolitical context.

12. But the context in which the Church routinely proclaims special revelation and redemption to the world is not civil government, but the ministry of evangelism from the pulpit, by person-to-person witness and visitation, and through the media. In this context of voluntary decision, in contrast to legislative-coercion, the Church is to herald the good news of the forgiveness of sins, new life in Christ, and the New Society ruled by Christ the risen Lord and returning Judge. Every social crisis that legislation addresses has its roots not primarily in the causes that sociologists tend to identify but rather in the loss of spiritual realities. At least five thousand young Americans, between ages fifteen and twenty-four, now commit suicide annually; some authorities place the figure at four times that number in view of the many deaths of young persons that police report as accidents. More than two hundred thousand young people now annually attempt suicide. Although adolescent distress over parental divorce, remarriage, and working mothers are conspicuous factors, secular sociologists tend to look to a congressionally created national prevention program for solution of the youth suicide problem. As Allan Carlson of The Rockford Institute comments, they project government research rather than a recovery of religion and traditional family life as the answer. The lowest suicide rate is in fact found where the nuclear family is intact; the highest, where parents are unmarried or divorced. Yet some religious activists both on the right and on the left look to political confrontation for a solution of pressing social concerns like abortion, teen suicide, and deviant lifestyles, while the Church, neglectful of her spiritual mission, is herself invaded by secular compromises.

To be sure, when government engages in programs that violate Christian conscience, such as funding abortions and denying free speech to evangelical students meeting on public school properties, bold protest is proper. But such protest gains one-sided political overtones when some churches approve abortion-on-demand and when evangelical students attending public schools show little interest either in voluntary prayer or in Bible study. The risk is that political policy will be looked upon to compensate for values that should be nurtured by parents at home and by the churches, while the importance of personal devotion and evangelism is neglected.

13. The Church is not to blame for the world's predicament, even if she needs a much more profound strategy of Christian evangelism and Christian public involvement. God has a plan for human history in which the regenerate Church is the center of hope and destiny—a plan that focuses on demonic influences and sin as the root problem and on redemption by Christ as the decisive solution. The dream of world-utopia that blurs the significance of sin and redemption in focusing the human predicament and its solution is a fantasy of nonbelievers. Nothing in the New Testament encourages the idea of world conversion. The American evangelical movement is an unusual historical marvel, and history may record that through short-sightedness evangelicals watched it self-destruct. In the world at large Christians of all kinds now number about 20 percent of the global population. A massive effort to double that number would still leave Christians a minority, with a new generation of infants being born daily. Atheism lacks resources to sustain the beggarly remnants of human value and hope that a fallen humanity retains. Nature loosed from God can be a causal mechanism that cancels human liberty and worth or it can be a planetary accident that humans may loot and ravage for personal advantage. History loosed from God can be a pattern of meaningless cycles, each turning inward, or an arena in which superman imagines himself to be its divine lord.

14. The Christian revelation gives substance to human hope. The world knows how to verbalize hope but misconstrues its meaning. As far back as the ancient Greeks, hope signaled an ambiguous outcome; one had to wait out its obscurities to learn if tomorrow brings fortune or misfortune. Christianity focuses hope on the sure triumph of God centered in the Lord's triumphant return. Hope for Christianity is not divorced from faith and reason, or from history. The forfeiture of hope is often the last blow before a person loses mental stability. In larger social context a pervasive melancholy often presages the breakdown of a culture.

Christianity offers a living hope, and sufficient reason for it. It carries assurance that God is at once Lord of the future and Sovereign of the present. That is all the reason one needs for confronting the ever-crumbling expectations of modernity with the enduring principles of Christianity.

PART TWO:

ESSENTIALS IN THE BATTLE FOR TRUTH

THE FIGHT OF THE DAY

The Apostle Paul is concerned lest we be asleep when we ought to be on guard duty. We have a fight on our hands, he says, and we need to be awake and primed for it. *Phillips Modern English Version* paraphrases his comments in Romans 13:11-14:

> The present time is of the highest importance—it is time to wake up to the reality. The night is nearly over, the day has almost dawned. Every day brings God's salvation nearer than the day in which we took the first step of faith. Let us therefore fling away the things that men do in the dark, let us arm ourselves for the fight of the day. . . . Let us be Christ's men from head to foot, and give no chance to the flesh to have its fling.

On my first night's sleep in Keruzawa, Japan, I had no idea that I was in an earthquake zone until a midnight jolt awakened me to reality. The tremor didn't register topmost on the Richter scale, but its severity reminded me nonetheless not to take tomorrow for granted. So these words of the apostle, in the middle of the epistle to the Romans, stab us awake and shock us alive to the invisible realities of the spiritual world, lest we be entrapped in a sinful, slumbering society.

Three emphases seem to me to rise from this text in our present life-situation: first, American culture is sinking toward sunset; second, Christian believers are stretching toward sunrise; and third, we are warriors with a mission in the world.

I. AMERICAN CULTURE IS SINKING TOWARD SUNSET

At the opening of the epistle, Paul unveils God's anger over the depths of Gentile rebellion. Three times we hear that dreadful refrain, "*God gave them over.*" We read that, because of their persistent wickedness, God "gave them over to the *sinful desires* of their hearts" (1:24, NIV), that God "gave them over to *shameful lusts*" (1:26, NIV), and that God "gave them over to *a depraved mind*" (1:28, NIV).

Exegetes have long noted a progression here: desires, lusts, mindset. As the channel of sin runs ever deeper, God's compensatory judgment moves ever closer to final abandonment and inescapable doom. The first chapter closes in fact with a warning of doomsday ahead for those who in their own consciences know that all who live wickedly deserve God's death penalty, yet who nonetheless defy God and even encourage others to do so (1:32).

I have a heavy heart about America. American culture seems to me to be sinking toward sunset. I do not, like some, call America the epicenter of evil in the world. But we have fallen far from lofty ideals for which this land came into being. I don't intend to spend most of my time reciting a catalogue of vices. Yet our country seems more and more to act out of traditional character. To be sure, there is a godly remnant—not simply a tiny band but a goodly number—for which we may be grateful. But it is surely not America at her best when we chart the massacre of a million unborn children a year, the flight from the monogamous family, two and a half million persons trapped in illegal drugs and alcohol (our country now has a larger drug problem than any other industrialized nation in the world), the normalizing of deviant sexual behavior (in the Washington-Baltimore area alone there are now estimated to be two hundred and fifty thousand homosexuals), the proliferation of AIDS to twenty-five thousand persons, more than half of whom have already died, with reportedly 10,000,000 infected with the virus.

What is underway is a redefinition of the good life, a redefinition that not only perverts the word "good" but perverts the term "life" as well. What is "good" is corrupted into whatever gratifies one's personal desires, whatever promotes self-interest even at the expense of the dignity and worth of others. In that fantasy-world of sinful desires, shameful lusts, and a depraved mind, sexual libertinism is good, coveting and stealing are good, violence and terrorism are good.

Worse yet, such perversion of the good is connected with what is called "the life." All that the Bible means by life—spiritual life, moral life, eternal life, a life fit for eternity—is emptied into an existence fit only for beasts and brutes.

"They gave up God," says Paul, "and therefore God gave them up—to be playthings of their own foul desires in dishonoring their own bodies." They "deliberately forfeited the truth of God and accepted a lie, paying homage and giving service to the creature instead of the Creator, who alone is worthy to be worshipped for ever and ever. God therefore handed them over to disgraceful passions" (Rom. 1:24-27, *Phillips*).

Western society is experiencing a great cultural upheaval. More and more the wicked subculture comes to open cultural manifestation. More and more the unmentionables become the parlance of our day. More and more profanity and vulgarity find expression through the mass media. The sludge of a sick society is rising to the top and, sad to say, the stench does not offend even some public leaders. Our nation increasingly trips the worst ratings on God's Richter scale of fully deserved moral judgment.

God who shook the earth at Sinai, God who shook the earth at Calvary, God who is a consuming fire warns of one more shaking, that final and decisive shaking: "Yet once more will I make to tremble not the earth only, but also the heaven. This means," as the author of Hebrews says, "that in this final 'shaking' all that is impermanent will be removed . . . and only the unshakable things will remain" (Heb. 12:26, 27, *Phillips*). The world will be asleep when doomsday comes, Peter warns, banking its life on the premise that "everything continues exactly as it has always been since the world began" (2 Pet. 3:4). "But the Day of the Lord will come," he emphasizes, "and the earth and all that is in it will be laid bare" (2 Pet. 3:10).

When that great meltdown comes, where will you be? Trapped in Sodom? In the bleak twilight of a decadent culture, where will you be? Overtaken, like Lot, looking back at the citadels of sin? "Wake up!" says Paul; "wake up!" American culture is sinking toward sunset.

II. Christian Believers Are Stretching Toward Sunrise

The remarkable thing about Paul's exhortation to awaken from sleep is that it is addressed to Christians. It apprises them not of encroaching doom but of daybreak, of the imminent sunrise, of the full dawning of God's Kingdom. "Let us arm ourselves for the fight of the day," he writes, "[and] be Christ's men from head to foot."

Christians have duties in the cultural upheaval around us. God has not told us to build an ark or to escape the floodwaters by taking to the hills. If there is hope for America, it will come through the vigorous proclamation and application of the Christian message.

The early Christians knew the fierceness of the battle. They knew Gentile wickedness at its worst; it was the moving spirit of the society in which they were reached for the gospel. "You were spiritually dead through your sins and failures, all the time that you followed this world's ideas of living and obeyed the evil ruler of the spiritual realm. . . . We all lived like that in the past," writes Paul, "and followed the desires and imaginings of our lower nature, being in fact under the wrath of God by nature, like everyone else. . . . We were dead in our sins" (Eph. 2:2, 3, *Phillips*).

Don't for a moment forget that we ourselves were dug from the sludge of a sick society. When recently I wrote *Confessions of a Theologian* it had a double exposure—first, on the world from which Christ rescues even those who become theologians and pastors and deacons, and second, on the world to which Christ lifted me, the eternal world to which he lifts prostitutes and drug addicts and homosexuals and other redeemed sinners. The risen Christ is in the moving and lifting business. How far has He removed you from the old life and lifted you to divine service? How high has Christ lifted you?

It is one thing to run away from sin; it is yet another to run up a flag for faith. "Fling away the things that men do in the dark," exhorts Paul, and "give no chance to the flesh to have its fling. . . . Be Christ's men from head to foot. . . . Let us arm ourselves for the fight of the day." God wants your mind. He wants your will. He wants your heart—the whole self. "Christ in you" is Paul's great theme in the letter to the Colossians. Where your feet go, does Christ walk with you? Where your mind reaches, is the mind of Christ yours also? In whatever your will embraces, is Christ's will astride your own?

During the days of the youth counterculture a lad went door to door asking, "Does Jesus Christ live here?" Taken aback, one housewife replied, "My husband's a deacon." The lad answered,

"That's not what I asked: Does Jesus Christ live here?" Christian believers are stretching toward sunrise. "Be Christ's men from head to foot"!

III. We Are Warriors with a Mission in the World

Christian duty requires of us more than personal piety and devotion, important as that is. It's not enough to say "no" when the culture holds that fornication is a morally acceptable option and that we may abort the unborn child if it's unwanted or take hallucinatory drugs if we are minded to do so.

Are you aware of the cultural challenges we face? Or are you yourself debilitated by the shoddy secular values of our time?

"*The fight of the day*"—are you aware of what that entails?

In the battle between good and evil, are you armed and engaged in "the fight of the day"?

In the battle for the minds of men, are you armed and engaged in "the fight of the day"?

In the battle for the will of humanity, are you armed and engaged in "the fight of the day"?

In the exhibition of a Christian mindset, are you armed and engaged in "the fight of the day"?

In the deployment of Christian countermoves, are you armed and engaged in "the fight of the day"?

Just as there are depths of depravity in human life, so too there are levels of dedication. And just as God progressively abandons renegades to their rebellion, so too He rewards the righteous in their spiritual renewal. When ancient Rome fell, it was the godly Christian remnant that walked head-high into the future. When medieval Christianity compromised its Biblical heritage, the Protestant Reformation emerged to bring great blessing to Europe and the world. When the post-Enlightenment era spawned an anti-Biblical mindset, the eighteenth-century evangelical awakening in England spared that nation the travesties of the French Revolution. What will be the final verdict on the evangelical confrontation of today's radically secular humanism? We are on the threshold of the decade of destiny, in the last generation before we leave behind the twentieth century, the end of one century and the beginning of another. What spiritual situation do we bequeath not only to those who follow us, but also to our contemporaries?

Christianity is qualitatively different or it has nothing distinctive to offer the world. The real arena in which we are to work and witness and win over others is the world, or we have ceased to be light, salt, leaven. Christian duty requires courageous participation at the frontiers of public concern—education, mass media, politics, law, literature and the arts, labor and economics, and the whole realm of cultural pursuits. We need to do more than to sponsor a Christian *subculture*. We need Christian *counterculture* that sets itself alongside the secular rivals and publishes openly the difference that belief in God and His Christ makes in the arenas of thought and action. We need Christian *countermoves* that commend a new climate, countermoves that penetrate the public realm. To live christianly involves taking a stand for God that calls this world's caesars to account before the sovereign Lord of the universe, that calls this world's sages to account before the wisdom that begins with the fear of the Lord, that calls this world's journalists to account before The Greatest Story Ever Told. We must strive to reclaim this cosmos for its rightful owner, God, who has title to the cattle on a thousand hills, and for Christ who says to the lost multitudes, "I made you; I died for you; I ransomed you."

What does that mean for the world of the liberal arts and the sciences? What does it imply for the mass media? What are its consequences for the political realm? What does it imply for the debate over human freedom and justice and rights?

We may not know all the answers, but we know some absolutes at least, and that puts us head and shoulders above the relativists, and the woods are full of relativists today. Each of us must find his or her proper station and platform in "the fight of the day" and use our God-given talent to reflect the truth and justice of God into the world of public affairs. Everywhere around us is strewn the philosophical wreckage of those who rely only on the voice of conscience, on social utility, on aesthetic gratification, on majority consensus—on everything but a sure Word of God. If you are still wavering between the God of the ages and the spirit of the age, listen to Paul's warning summons. American culture is sinking toward sunset. Christian believers are stretching toward sunrise. We are warriors with a mission in the world. Have you enlisted, winsomely and courageously, in what Paul calls "the fight of the day"?

BEGGARS AND BENEFACTORS

Let me set the record straight. When speaking of beggars, I am not here referring either to street people or to professional fund-raisers, not even to television evangelists. Nor am I criticizing or commending beggars as a class. Sometimes begging may be a necessity, perhaps even a virtue.

Some years ago, in Portland, Oregon, after I had preached, two women in their thirties came to greet me. "We are domestics," one said, "and work for very rich people." "Please pray for them," she added. "They can buy anything they want," she continued. "They don't know what it is to have to receive something as a gift." The gift they had in mind, of course, was God's great gift of redemptive grace in Christ. Only those who come as needy suppliants receive the priceless gift of divine salvation.

Even we Christians can self-sufficiently take for granted life in the Spirit as a daily-renewed gift. And we easily forget also that the food and shelter we routinely accept contrasts with the daily experience of multitudes who have no idea where tomorrow's bread will come from, if there is any. Those who need to beg for what others take for granted know how truly wonderful such things are, and know the excitement and joy of obtaining them.

Many years ago I was speaking at First Baptist Church in Detroit for Dr. Hillyer Stratton. I arrived Saturday night by train and walked to the nearby hotel. On the way I passed a used book store and ended up buying as many volumes as I could carry. The next day after the morning service the agent at the Detroit train station refused to sell me a ticket to Chicago because I was a few cents short and Traveler's Aid was closed. Loaded with more books than luggage, I walked shyly through the waiting room begging for a few pennies, hoping that none of the millionaires I had just preached to were nearby. Never in my life did a bit of change look more precious than when I tried to extract a few small coins from skeptical and unresponsive travelers. One man finally gave me a dime, and I was on my way with change to spare.

I don't know whether you have ever had to beg. The experience, let me assure you, has some spiritual values. Those of us who have once been poor often sense the value of what others take for granted; we know both the need for something and the joy of receiving it, and hopefully also some of the joy of sharing it.

Jesus says something remarkable about begging and giving. In open view of the multitudes Jesus instructs His disciples. In immediate context the disciples' mission is local, temporary, and restricted to Israel. But Jesus was preparing those disciples for a universal and permanent mission that would embrace the Gentiles as well.

> So Jesus went round all the towns and villages, preaching in their synagogues, announcing the good news of the Kingdom, and curing every kind of ailment and disease. The sight of the people moved him to pity; they were like sheep without a shepherd, harassed and helpless; and he said to his disciples, 'The crop is heavy, but labourers are scarce; you must therefore beg the owner to send labourers to harvest his crop.' Then he called his twelve disciples and gave them authority to cast out unclean spirits and to cure every kind of ailment and disease. (Matt. 9:35—10:1, NEB)

Many facets of this text are controversially in the limelight today: divine healing, unclean spirits, apostolic gifts. But I focus on two emphases: first, a harvest so ripe for reaping that Jesus instructs His disciples to beg the Lord of harvest for workers; second, the concerned disciples whom the Lord in turn dispatches as authorized harvesters.

First: a critical historical situation establishes the urgency of proclaiming the gospel, and the disciples are to implore God because of this dire plight of the masses. They are not simply to brief the Lord about fields white unto harvest; they are to shoulder a personal concern for reapers and to beg Him to send forth harvesters.

The versions most familiar to us translate *deomai* by "pray"— "pray the Lord of the harvest." But since prayer so often becomes perfunctory, the word "beg" in *The New English Bible* under-scores and intensifies the urgency of the appeal. The same Greek verb occurs in Acts 4:31 where the early Church, harassed by religious oppression, begged for God's help until the gathering-place shook and they were filled with the Holy Spirit and with boldness. A further step in ministry is to pray not for one's self and one's own fortunes, but for others. The worker whose heart God stretches to embrace the plight of Planet Earth is the worker who begs God in behalf of human need, the worker who pleads the cause of the lost and beleaguered, who wrestles the cause of unreached multitudes. He begs God for the filling of impoverished pulpits, begs for the integrity of Christian colleges and seminaries, begs for political leaders of honest courage, begs for bold Christian witness in an age of secular humanism.

We find the term *deomai* again in 2 Corinthians 5:20. The Apostle Paul declares that we are "ambassadors for Christ, as though God were beseeching you through us; we beg (*deometha*) you in Christ's behalf, be reconciled to God." Just as earnestly as God is entreated to send workers, just so earnestly the lost world is begged in turn to become reconciled to God. An unmistakable spiritual connection exists between the sense of urgent harvest that implores God for workers and the sense of urgency with which the commissioned worker himself reaches out to the beleaguered world.

This, then, is my second and final emphasis: the beggars become the benefactors. Nor only does the God of the eternal decrees build prayer into His creation as a means to advance His purposes, but He also responds to the needs of lost humanity by dispatching the very workers who know what it is to beg for the rebellious world's reconciliation to God. The Greek word here used for "send"—"beg the owner to send"—is *ekballo,* to thrust forth. The solicitous laborers are launched into their mission by a divine thrust. In this last segment of the twentieth century, don't let Challenger astronauts take the only risks of propulsion into the future.

To the variety of human need in this world God matches a remarkable task force and vast range of means. One preaches, another teaches, another writes, another translates, another transports, another builds. The Great Reaper advances His overarching purpose through multiplied harvesters who seldom see how seemingly minute efforts blend ultimately into some bold redemptive victory. As Jesus says in the parable of the landowner (Matt. 20:1), we are "laborers who farm for the owners of the land." Each of us reaps part of the harvest in an interdependent effort. The divine thrust involves many booster rockets that set Christ's cause fully into orbit.

We are to beg the Lord of the universe not because prayer can manipulate God, or because it has merely an internal subjective value as a spiritual discipline. Prayer is one of the means God has etched into the cosmos for the advancement of His purposes. Recall the excellent Article (116) on prayer in the Heidelberg Catechism, especially the words: "God will give His grace and Holy Spirit to those only who with hearty sighing unceasingly beg them of Him and thank Him for them." Fervent intercession is declared the means of God's bestowal of the gifts of grace. The divine benefactions are for "those only" who "with hearty sighing unceasingly beg them of Him and thank Him for them."

Even Old Testament critical scholarship has now rediscovered the prophet's role as intercessor, begging God in behalf of Israel even before publicly declaring God's impending judgment. Not until God commands him no longer to pray for the nation's rescue does Jeremiah desist from prayer for Israel. Ezekiel's intercession too is divinely interrupted. Intercessory prayer is an indicator of how deeply we are involved in the concerns and fortunes of others. Those who are beggars of God in turn become benefactors holding before impoverished humanity the forgiveness of sins, the meaning of life, the cause of justice, the abiding riches of eternity. That mission falls to us at a time when multitudes demean the glory of the living God; when His call for social justice is widely spurned; when His inspired Book is questioned, even in His own house; when the gospel of grace is all too often blurred and the Christian worldview truncated. It is the beggars of God who become God's benefactors to mankind.

To your knees, then, when, as Solzhenitsyn says, "men have forgotten God"; to your knees when secular humanism spurns the supernatural; to your knees when the once-Christian West outruns its moral capital and risks spiritual bankruptcy; to your knees when history is at a decisive parting of the ways; to your knees when the civilizational mindset is yielding to culture in chaos; to your knees when the churches' light grows dim while America needs a new will and courage for the right.

In God's job description the benefactor and the beggar are

one and the same. No benefactor ever touched greater glory than when begging God to bestow His grace upon lost mankind. And no beggar ever reveled in greater rewards than when God thrusts him into an impoverished world as a dispenser of divine riches. "*Beg,* . . . that he will *send.*"

ARE THEOLOGIANS AN ENDANGERED SPECIES?

> Be diligent to present yourself approved to God as a work-
> man who does not need to be ashamed, handling accurately
> the word of truth. (2 Tim. 2:15, NASB)

In our generation it is easier to say what constitutes an endangered species than to define a theologian.

Everyone has a theology, we say routinely, albeit often a shab-
by one. But in any case that does not make everyone a theologian.
Usually we mean by the term *theologian* a student of theology or a
specialist in theology. But not every student of theology is a
theologian, and some specialists in theology would assure us that
God is dead.

Fortunately the Apostle Paul was spared such modern circum-
locutions. He exhorts young Timothy to "be diligent to present
yourself approved to God as a workman who does not need to be
ashamed, handling accurately the word of truth" (2 Tim. 2:15,
NASB). The faithful laborer whose work is theology will inherit
this concern to "cut straight" the Word of Truth, to expound it
undistorted and unperverted, so that before God he may stand
unashamed and approved. The venerable King James Version renders *orthotomeō* as "rightly dividing"—not subtracting from the
Word of Truth, or adding to it, but rightly exposing human
thought, decision, and life to its cutting edge.

Theologians are indeed an endangered species, and for three
reasons.

First, theologians are prone to champion the tradition of the
elders. That need not always be a bad thing. An anchorless generation like our own, adrift from its moral and spiritual heritage,
pays a high penalty for its existential vagabondage. Yet it takes

one's breath away to read the Gospels and to note that Jesus reserved some of His most caustic criticism for the theologians of his day. "Woe unto you, scribes and Pharisees," He warns (Matt. 23:13), linking the trusted interpreters of the Hebrew Scriptures with the self-righteous professionals who splintered the divine imperatives into negotiable fragments and then claimed to fulfill the law's demands. The scribes, like the Pharisees, "love the place of honor at banquets and the chief seats in the synagogues," He warned, "and respectful greetings in the market place, and being called by men, Rabbi" (Matt. 23:6ff.); "hypocrites," He rebuked them, "for you devour widow's houses, even while for a pretense you make long prayers" (23:14); moreover, you regard "the gold of the temple" as more important than "the temple that sanctified it" (23:16ff.), and are concerned with tithing more than with justice and mercy and faithfulness (23:23) and pursue a good public image while practicing self-indulgence (23:25). "I say to you," Jesus told His followers, "unless your righteousness surpasses that of the scribes and Pharisees, you shall not enter the kingdom of heaven" (Matt. 5:20).

Theologians are indeed a vulnerable species. "Woe unto you, scribes . . . " is hardly a motto that the Evangelical Theological Society would eagerly adopt. But the words carry enduring warning that we who divide the Word of Truth can distort and pervert it to our shame and thus invite divine disapproval. You and I carry in ourselves the same latent propensities, the same possibilities for spiritual miscarriage, that made those earlier carriers of a sacred tradition an endangered company.

It is "the word of truth" that we are called to champion; let the chips of tradition fall where they may. It is for divine approval that we are to strive earnestly, to be diligent like an artisan skillfully plying his craft. Although the King James Version has "*Study* to show yourself approved," that is not the best rendering. Yet the probing of Scripture remains our continuing duty. Jesus exhorted the blundering Jewish leaders to "search the Scriptures, for they are they which testify of me" (John 5:39), and the Apostle Paul, who was "a Pharisee of the Pharisees," would later contrast the "traditions of men" (Col. 2:8) with the prophetic word (Rom. 1:2) and the inspired tradition relayed by the apostles (2 Thess. 2:15). We are to familiarize ourselves with the totality of the divinely-given Word, with the whole counsel of God; we are to explore and investigate it. In the *Gulag Archipelago* Alexander Solzhenitsyn tells of Soviet police conducting a house search, and he comments, "They left nothing untouched." Let not our evangelical or Reformed tradition as such be our hallmark, but let the Word of Biblical truth constitute our tradition. Theologians who stand solely with a revered tradition are always an endangered species.

Secondly, theologians face the ready temptation to think that the schematic system or speculative philosophy they bring to the Bible is what makes the Judeo-Christian revelation and faith in God specially credible. Contemporary theology illustrates this vulnerability on a massive scale. It may not find the key to the Scriptures in Mary Baker Eddy's *Science and Health,* but it hails Whiteheadean process philosophy, Bultmannian existentialism, the theology of revolution, or some other distinctively modern approach as giving Christianity a new lease on life.

The theologian is imperiled as well as his theological enterprise if he thinks Biblical theism depends for its credibility and power upon speculative discoveries and disclosures peculiar to our century, or to any century this side of the apostolic age. "The word of truth" of which Paul writes is a divine given; it is not a tentative proposal awaiting human reorientation, whether through a system made in Marburg or Claremont or, let me add, on Chestnut Hill or in Arlington, Virginia. It is Scripture that illumines the contemporary conjectural conceptualities far more than these current speculative insights confer credibility upon the Bible.

Theologians are an endangered species when they consider theology merely a human construct, a creative enterprise in which mankind projects upon the invisible world an explanatory model that hopefully provides a coherent grasp of ultimate reality or an inner psychological gratification. But the idea of God originates with God, not with mankind; it is God who takes the initiative in His self-disclosure, who universally makes Himself intelligibly known, and who gives theology its authoritative foundation in Scripture.

It is little wonder that some who focus on theology as essentially a human enterprise have in our century called for an end to preaching and verbalization and call instead for concentration on

Christian social concerns. The world, they say, is weary of words and famished for deeds; theology, they insist, can now be done effectively only by works that speak louder than words.

All of us, I am sure, applaud evangelical social engagement. But had there been no apostolic proclamation while the apostles day and night, month after month performed good works, not even the most disciplined empiricist could have extracted from their behavior such conclusions as the incarnation of the Logos, the sinlessness of Jesus and His substitutionary atonement for sinners, His bodily resurrection and impending return in glory and judgment. When contemporary theologians call for works and not words, there is reason to believe that some are less interested in a supernatural faith that works than they are in circumventing the apostolic kerygma.

Beware then of the creative theologian who claims to bring to the Bible some updated framework that confers credibility on Biblical theology. Scripture is credible as it stands; it is "the word of truth" that needs only to be "cut straight." The theologian is endangered not only by the tradition of the elders, as I have already said. He is endangered also by the speculation of contemporaries whose efforts to administer "first aid" to the Scriptural view are but inadequate and artificial life supports.

Let me mention a third and final danger, not related to our elders or to our contemporaries as much as to ourselves. We theologians become a self-endangered species when we leash our message to ghettos of faith and do not unleash it into the world for which it was intended. Christianity is good news for Planet Earth; if we confine its convictions to the churches, we will needlessly forfeit its cultural impact to naturalistic alternatives. We need to stake a claim to the air waves and the media, to the educational arena and to the political realm. Timidity in addressing the civilizational and cultural frontiers in a constructively critical way poses great peril to theologians and to theology. Isolate ourselves and we suggest that our message and we the messengers are irrelevant to the world in which God has placed us.

To be sure, much that passes for evangelical social involvement today leaves my uneasy conscience almost as uneasy as did evangelical noninvolvement—its triumphal and confrontational spirit, its exaggeration of a support base, its ready exploitation of the moral crisis for personal promotion, and its defamation as enemies of fellow-Americans and even fellow-Christians who may not share every article of a preannounced political agenda. But much as I wish evangelicals would put their house in order, I see no basis for deploring the religious right as disruptive of national unity; I regard the reentry of fundamentalists into the public arena as desirable; and I am wholly committed—not indeed to a Christian (let alone Islamic) theocracy, or to a quasi-official humanistic or atheistic religion—but to the propriety of a Christian nation as an expression of religious voluntarism. But American evangelicalism is forfeiting historical opportunities in our time, and some may never return, as in the launching of a great metropolitan evangelical university.

We must not be held at bay by the powers of this world, or defanged by the spirit of our age. We dare not grant the finality of the present world-establishment, or to seek only minor modifications of it. Give that world-spirit your little finger and your body and soul will soon also go with it.

In America and in Western Europe the wolf of secular humanism almost everywhere crouches at the door. Despite all that has been said about an evangelical awakening, a humanist aura still overarches the academic world, the political arena, and the mass media. The mood and mentality of our age is slipping towards raw naturalism; the sexual preoccupation of ancient Pompeii overarches the entertainment and recreational world; fornication and abortion have become almost as routine as going to the supermart. Multitudes of young girls barely in their teens become mothers of unwanted infants; alcohol and dope addiction have become high school vices. We read of a mother dismembering and then discarding her own daughter; of teachers and baby-sitters and even a priest sexually abusing young children. We read of prison conditions so vile that they deteriorate rather than rehabilitate offenders; of homeless street people coping with subzero weather. This occurs not in pre-Christian pagan Rome, but in this our own land, the land to which Edwards and Finney and Moody and Graham have proclaimed the evangel and whose fifty million evangelicals dispatch missionaries around the globe.

Speak to the conscience of this nation. Speak in the name of the holy God of the universe. Speak in the name of Biblical justice. Speak in the name of Scriptural compassion. Speak in the name of Jesus Christ. Let the world know that the authentic theologian is a person of spiritual vision, moral integrity, and high courage, one who refuses to be intimidated by the tradition of the elders (even if it be an evangelical establishment and its power brokers), one who refuses to be detoured by contemporary religious speculation, one who refuses through provincial platitudes to allow the theologians to become an endangered species.

Our theology must be done in empathetic solidarity with all for whom Christ died. It must have an eye to the morally wicked and bankrupt, the spiritually lost, the centers of power and the destitute and oppressed, and for the learned who substitute the traditions of academe for the revelation of Yahweh. It must dispute the prevalent notion of self-fulfillment, which snubs evangelical new birth as regressive.

We need a missiological theology alert to all the frontiers of human tragedy, abreast of the competing worldviews and confused cultures of our age. Our theology must embrace not only our continent whose poverty is specially focused in material aggrandizement and sexual libertinism, but a larger world also that accommodates unmitigated famine and unrelieved destitution, that copes with Islamic terrorism and Koranic or Soviet expansionism. We need a theology aware that during your lifetime, given present trends, fewer Christians may live on the northern half of our planet than in Africa, Asia and Latin America. We need a theology braced for the collapse of contemporary civilization while it holds aloft the Christ of redemptive revelation as the only enduring ground of freedom and holy joy.

May it be said of us that we had no need to be ashamed, that in our time we cut straight the Word of Truth, and that we diligently sought God's approval as the workmen we were divinely called to be.

SEVEN

THE CREATOR AND THE NEO-PAGAN MIND

I

The other day I read a book that makes one's hair stand on end. Not that it's pornographic. It's an old book—centuries old—but it so pointedly anticipates modern neo-paganism that it's startling. I speak of *Ecclesiastes*.

Take, for example, chapter 1:4-7: "The sun goes down and hastens to the place where it arose. . . . The rivers flow into the sea . . . and from thence they return again." Everything turns in upon itself; everything is a meaningless cycle. This doctrine of eternal recurrence, ancient as it is, is rearing its head again.

Then there's 2:11 and 2:18 on the futility of work: I looked at all my labor and it was "a grasping for the wind." And 3:16 on the relativity of ethical judgments: in the halls of justice there is wickedness, and in the place of righteousness, iniquity; everywhere right and wrong are manipulated, good and evil reduced to personal preferences.

Again, 3:18-30: human beings are essentially animals—even if a little more complex; the same fate befalls them both, and the grave is man's final destiny. "As one dies, so dies the other. . . . They all have one breath; man has no advantage over the animals. . . . All go to one place; all are from the dust, and all return to dust." Or take 8:14, 15: human history is meaningless; it has no enduring purpose. "There are just men to whom it happens according to the work of the wicked; again, there are wicked men to whom it happens according to the work of the righteous." History is not patterned by an ethical or moral goal. And take that classic declaration that, given the nature of things, the shrewd lifestyle, the way to stay on top, is to "eat, drink and be merry, for tomorrow we die"; as 8:15 puts it, "I commend enjoyment, because a man has nothing better under the sun than to eat, drink and be merry; for this will remain with him in his labor all the days of his life."

It reeks with modern humanism, doesn't it?—or worse yet, with the raw mood of unadulterated paganism: naturalism which has lost its humanism, the rancid neo-paganism that even now lurks around the corner of contemporary Western philosophy.

II

Now if you think that the writer of Ecclesiastes commends and teaches these doctrines you profoundly misunderstand him. He identifies this pagan creed only to confront it and to reply to it. Ecclesiastes does not teach the theory that there is no meaning to life and to the universe except as we invent a meaning. He holds that there is objective meaning to life and history and the cosmos, though we may not know it; yet God knows it and, moreover, God reveals it.

The book has not merely a pagan undercurrent against which it contends and above which it rises, but has two subclimaxes in chapters 5 and 8 and then crescendos finally to its great culmination in chapter 12, "Remember your Creator in the days of your youth" before at last you meet spirit-to-Spirit with the God of moral judgment: "Fear God and keep His commandments. . . . For God will bring every work into judgment, including every secret thing, whether good or evil" (12:13, 14).

In 5:1 the author pleads, "Come to the house of God" and "listen to the Word of God"; in 5:19, 20 he exhorts, "live life with joy as the gift of God." And again in 5:12, 13 he warns that God will stand with the righteous but that the wicked are doomed.

III

In the grand closing chapter Solomon urges that we remember the Creator at the earliest opportunity in life, "before the evil days come" or "the years draw nigh in which thou shalt have no pleasure in them." Note that life moves toward a terrible future for those who neglect to put life right with the Creator.

Ecclesiastes emphasizes three things: first, that no one can be truly successful in life without having found spiritual success; second, that in order to find spiritual success one need not wait until old age or middle age, but one can walk with the Creator in the early years; finally, that not to find spiritual success has calamitous consequences, not only in the life to come, but in this life also, as one moves through the crisis-experiences common to all human beings.

Solomon warns us that the pagan option is always knocking at the door of the person who crowds God out of his or her life. In six short verses he pictures human life as a house beaten by furious storms. This house is fragile; it will not last forever. It is the common lot of mankind that severe storms and crackling winds sweep over this aging edifice; accident and affliction, deterioration and disease are aspects of our finite existence. When those thunderclouds and wild winds strike, it makes a day-or-night difference whether in advance of them one has or has not entered into a right relationship with his Creator. The same experiences that drive the trusting believer closer to God will drive the unbeliever further away from Him.

The writer speaks, in verse 2, of the psychic side of life before he goes on to speak of the physical. "Remember your Creator . . . before the sun and the light, the moon and the stars are darkened." There are lights around this house: the light of the mind, of conscience, of imagination. They are all very fragile; the powers of reason fade, conscience grows dim, and the powers of imagination run wild. Give your mind to God, let the Creator enliven your conscience, he pleads, before the lights that illumine this house give way. Think God's thoughts after Him before reason runs riot and conscience is seared by the evils of this world.

Then, in verses 3-7, he speaks of the physical side of life: all the fragile facets of bodily survival are pummeled and stressed by the wild storms that beat upon us in this earthly life.

Remember your Creator, he says, "before the day when the keepers of the house shall tremble, and the strong (ones) shall bow themselves" (v. 3a). There are girders and supportive beams in this house, and they too will give way. The keepers of the house are the hands; when at last they tremble, they no longer are able to keep man in room and board. I have seen artists and cabinet-makers and painters suddenly lose their usefulness to themselves and to society as the keepers of the house begin to tremble and the strong girders—the arms and limbs—bow down or give way. It makes a world of difference then whether in the earlier years one has remembered his Creator. The ungodly man blames and curses God ("if there were a God He would not let this happen to me") in the very same circumstances that drive the godly man closer to His Creator ("He has not failed me before; He will not fail me now").

The very same experience will drive one closer to and the other further away from God as pagan naturalism moves energetically into a vacuum and spiritual rebellion allies itself with all the bitter complaints that Ecclesiastes echoes as the ungodly man seeks to justify his spiritual failure.

Remember your Creator, says Ecclesiastes, "before the grinders cease because they are few and those that look out of the windows grow dim" (v. 3b). Grinders, as you know, is the Old Testament term for teeth. When the teeth gave way, the ancients did not have partials and plates, and the mill at the gate of the house couldn't function. Remember your Creator before "the doors are shut in the streets and the sound of the grinding is low" (v. 4a). When one finds the fullness of life only in whatever one can stoke into the pantry, what does the creed "eat, drink and be merry" amount to if the chore of eating itself becomes high tragedy? The man who knows his Creator will think of a resurrection life to come; the pagan blames God for abandoning him in the only life he has, and of depriving him of sensual enjoyment. And there are windows in this aging house: "those that look out of the windows"—that is, the eyes—will grow dim. One by one the senses give way—taste, sight, hearing: "all the daughters of music are brought low" (v. 4b)—voice and hearing alike.

Remember your Creator, pleads Solomon, before "the almond tree shall blossom" (v. 5). There's a tree planted by this house—an almond tree, which blossoms white in winter—and it is already blossoming snow-white for some. We moderns dye it or hide it, but God sees it, and we know it, for that whitening crown indicates that human life is moving toward an end-time.

Remember your Creator, the writer pleads, before "the grasshopper is a burden, and desire fails, for man goes to his eternal home, and the mourners go about the streets" (v. 7). He doesn't mean only that life becomes such a chore that even an insect leaping across one's path is a nuisance. For things get worse and worse for this aging human, bent and twisted like a grasshopper—

knees stuck out, elbows back. Hunched over and moving like a grasshopper, he bears the burdens of the long years without anyone to share the load. In Isaiah 53:4, a great messianic passage, we read of Messiah, "surely He has borne our griefs and carried our sorrows." But this man has nobody to bear his burdens. His revolt against God is now almost second-nature; he wouldn't know divinity if it bit him in the foot. The evil days and the pleasureless years have come, and man "goes to his long home" (his eternal home), and this man senses that it is not the home of which Jesus later spoke when He said: "I go to prepare a place for you." "The mourners go about in the streets"—or as we would say, "the mortuary is right around the corner." He doesn't want to go, and he doesn't want to stay, for what is there to stay for, and what is there to go for?

Then Solomon makes a last high appeal. "Remember your Creator . . . before ever the silver cord is loosed, or the golden bowl is broken, or the pitcher is shattered at the fountain, or the wheel broken at the well. . . ." Even the ancient Hebrew rabbis understood this as a picture of the four ways in which death usually comes to a human being: the silver cord loosed, or the severing of the spinal cord; the golden bowl broken, or the brain ceasing to function; the pitcher shattered at the fountain, or the heart giving way; and the wheel broken at the well, or the loss of blood. Remember your Creator, he pleads, *before, before, before,* "for then will the dust return to the earth as it was, but the spirit will return to God who gave it" (v. 7).

Decision-time is over. Accounting-time has come. The pagan who said that there is no fixed truth, no final good, that man is a soulless beast and that purpose and meaning are private illusions, and that God is a myth, stands for judgment at last before the one true and living God, the moral Lord of the universe, the Chief Justice and Arbiter of human destiny.

Now is the time to put life right with Him, says Ecclesiastes. Every day without Him becomes a pagan interlude that all too soon preempts the whole of life on earth and, along with it, fixes one's eternal destiny. Remember, remember . . . at the earliest opportunity that remains . . . to come to terms with the Lord and Giver of life, a life intended for a daily walk on earth with Him, and for an eternity in His presence in the age to come.

PART THREE:

ILLUSION, IDEALISM AND BIBLICAL TRUTH

EIGHT

FEED THEM ON FANTASIES

The defect of liberation theology lies in the way it conceives and proposes to remedy the human predicament.

By no means is the projection of a new humanity and of a society in which justice and peace prevail an illegitimate venture. Its deepest roots, in fact, lie in the Bible. Whoever considers the politico-economic *status quo* sacred or normative, or uncritically resigns himself to it, needs to reread the Scriptures.

1. There are different species or varieties of liberation theology, but the genus to which they all belong is sociological rather than theological. The term is capable—as are most terms—of semantic manipulation. Liberation is, to be sure, a positive Biblical motif, whereas revolution is not an acceptable salvific catalyst. Liberation theology can therefore be made compatible with Christianity by emphasizing that Jesus is the Liberator and that the God of the Bible seeks liberation of the poor and the oppressed. But, for all that, liberation theology is not identical with Biblical "salvation theology." It embraces violence as a means of social change, even if—in distinction from revolution theology—it does so only as a last resort if other means fail. It therefore shares with the theology of revolution the conviction that revolutionary means may be necessary to transform society in an ideal way.

2. Liberation theology is for still another reason a stepchild of revolution theology rather than a legitimate offspring of salvation theology. It erroneously views the human predicament in terms of class struggle. In so doing it superimposes upon Scripture a Marxist analysis of human history that calls for Marxist solutions. A Scripturally acceptable liberation theology would need to exclude from its notion of liberation all such ideological misconceptions. The fact that liberation theology breaks with the radical materialism of Marxist-Leninist ideology—especially with the notion that history is ruled by deterministic laws and that history and society

alone determine what man is—does not of itself make the theory Biblical. For it proposes nonetheless to change the world by Marxist sociology. Much Marxist social science today avoids reference to Marx and Marxism, but Marxist analysis and supposed solution nonetheless covertly prevail. Christianity, however, has no license or need to borrow from or build upon the world's analysis of the human condition.

3. Because liberation theology thus reads the Bible through ideological lenses—as does revolution theology—it provides a masked religious front for a long-entrenched modernist socioeconomic agenda. When Protestant liberalism lost theological credibility, it deteriorated into a politico-economic program. The recent appeal to the Bible in behalf of both revolution and liberation theology reinvests this program with a divine sanction. It achieves a transformation of theology more than a transformation of society. It should therefore be unsurprising that its champions feel more at home in pluralistic ecumenical than in consistently evangelical contexts.

Instead of repressing religion as in earlier decades, revolutionary forces now increasingly deploy it to promote their socioeconomic goals. Cloaking Marxist revolution in the symbols of Christianity has become trendy since Castro's regime in Cuba; today Christianity is similarly exploited in Nicaragua. In his early years the late Archbishop William Temple held that socialism "is the economic realization of the Christian Gospel."[1] Many Western churchmen still think so, despite the abysmal failures of that system. The appeal to "*theology* of liberation" obscures the shift from theology to politics and economics as the catalytic agents of social change.

Liberation becomes the main rubric, theology a subordinate qualifying element. This is evident in the growing use of theological argument to support the political left in Europe, as well as in Latin America and elsewhere. The attainment of religious salvation is declared impossible without the improvement of economic and social conditions. The political transformation of seminaries and churches follows routinely.

4. There is no basis in the New Testament for considering *present* political liberation an integral facet of the gospel. The readiness to resort to violence (even if as a last resort) in quest of social justice not only breeds counterviolence, but it reflects an infatuation with contemporary utopia that has no Biblical sup-

ports. For the Church thus to elevate politico-economic sanctification to centrality is to cease to be the evangelical Church. If the achievement of present political liberation is a requirement of authentic fulfillment of the Great Commission, then has not the gospel been a failure and the Great Commission futile? It is a mistaken Jewish notion that the absence of universal peace and justice disqualifies Jesus as Messiah; it is remarkable that some contemporary Catholic and Protestant activists unwittingly lend credence to this misunderstanding. The Marxist belief in a presently attainable utopia is a misdirected inheritance from the Christian view of the future. The pursuit of and misexpectation of a contemporary paradise fosters unrealistic political and economic expectations and merely feeds starving souls on extravagant fantasies. Such a monumental hoax can only breed terrible disillusionment.

5. Liberation theology espouses an objectionable principle of Biblical interpretation. The hermeneutical principle affirmed by evangelical theology is christological, not sociological. The New Testament exalts Jesus Christ as superior to and supreme over every political ideology and activity promoting ethical and cultural change. For liberation philosophy, political involvement is more important than personal virtue; it becomes the test of Christian authenticity. But for the Church everything turns on the Lordship of Christ, not on political liberation; the former does not depend ontologically on the latter, even if it ultimately implies the latter. How do the life and example of the Jesus of history actually (not merely "symbolically"—symbols are capable of rival cognitive explanations) support the idea of a violent Jesus who as such is a forerunner of Marx and Mao? Or the notion that "radical discipleship" requires an insistent call not merely for sociopolitical justice but especially for the forced replacement of existing institutions by just alternatives? The whole tide of New Testament scholarship is against the view that Jesus was a Zealot seeking the overthrow of Rome. Jesus sponsored no programmatic attack on Roman political structures.

6. The notion that liberation theology makes the Bible and Christianity credible to the twentieth century is especially pernicious. The Bible needs to be understood for what it is and says; it is credible as it stands, apart from the superimposition of any scheme of speculative philosophy or political program or economic scheme. Those who impose an updated interpretative lens on

the Bible share in an ongoing process that destines their own alternative to inevitable replacement.

7. For a Third Age of the Spirit championed by earlier millennial enthusiasts, political theology substitutes a Final Paradise of Mammon, of materialistic abundance for all through an equalization of wealth. Yet neither Jesus nor the disciples bettered themselves financially as a direct consequence of their message. Many saints at Jerusalem lived on the edge of poverty, relieved by the voluntary gifts of believers elsewhere. The Bible does not make communism a badge of Christian authenticity. In the Middle Ages some devout Christians could even find spiritual merit in a vow of poverty. Modern political theology tends to promote interest in a Bread-and-Butter regime which Jesus in the feeding of the five thousand distinguished from His own intention.

None of these comments disputes the need for an energetic social application of Biblically-revealed principles. But a durable alternative to social injustices must flow from a Biblical view of the human predicament and of human rescue. Rejection of a revolutionary Christ or of a liberationist Christ does not require a passive Jesus; what it requires is an evangelical alternative. Evangelicals must break out of their cultural ghetto to demand social change, affirm that a better social order is possible in our own time, however preliminarily provisional and perfectible it remains in relation to the coming Kingdom of God. Not to elaborate that alternative will enable the champions of socialism, however self-defeating that option actually is, to win the war of ideas by default.

PERSPECTIVES ON CAPITAL PUNISHMENT

As neo-paganism increases, the value of human life diminishes, and the demand accelerates for the elimination of capital punishment.

A moral imperative obliges civil government to punish crime and, more than that, obliges the state also to enforce capital punishment under highly limited conditions. Hebrew theocratic government no longer exists, but the divine enjoinment of capital punishment antedated the Mosaic law and the Hebrew theocracy and remains in force. One reason law has lost its power in modern life is the failure to recognize divine law as the fundamental law. Modern states are, of course, free to compromise and ignore divine law, but they do so at their own peril.

The Bible grounds certain moral imperatives in God's universal creation ethic and others in His special salvation-covenant with Israel. The Genesis creation account affirms that all human beings bear God's created image, that God wills their propagation through monogamous marriage, and that God prescribes a work ethic.

The classic text on capital punishment (Gen. 9:6), which enjoins the death penalty for murder, likewise predates Moses and the Hebrew theocracy. It reinforces universal respect for the sanctity of human life by dooming a murderer to forfeit his life for destroying that of a fellow-human made in God's image. The sanctity of human life is guaranteed not simply by God's original creation of it, but also by a relationship to Him in which all human beings stand perpetually in distinction from the animal world.

Although God did not openly enjoin the death penalty until after the Noahic flood, Cain seems already to have feared death as a penalty for his murder of Abel (Gen. 4:14ff.). God protected Cain by expulsion, not because his act of murder was undeserving of death, but presumably to establish even the worth of the murderer's life against arbitrary blood vengeance. The Mosaic legislation later also prohibited blood vengeance. The Mosaic sixth commandment, "thou shalt not kill," carries forward the Noahic prohibition of murder. The law of retribution in the Old Testament, stipulating the limits of punishment, allowed the taking of "life for life" (Exod. 21:23ff.).

Although the Noahic passage (Gen. 9:6) might be read as an indicative description that the blood of the murdered "will be shed," this consequence is more naturally understood as a divinely mandated penalty in view of the preceding phrase (9:5): "I (God) will require the life of man" (cf. Ezek. 33:16; Deut. 18:9).

The Old Testament distinguishes deliberate, premeditated, intentional murder from negligent homicide and accidental manslaughter, and stipulates lesser penalties in such cases. But capital punishment is not declared always mandatory even when the killing of a human is intentional, as when a thief is overtaken in an act of theft or when there are not two witnesses who agree in their testimony. Hence not all murder requires the death penalty. Scripture in any case assumes the moral responsibility of the offender; it speaks of man as bearer of the divine image and hence as able to make rational and moral distinctions. It does not, therefore, preclude an alternative to capital punishment in the case of psychological, psychiatric or neurological disorder. If no previous indication of such disorder exists, however, the extended confinement of the offender seems, apart from medical cure, the only safeguard against spontaneous repetition of the crime.

The argument that Jesus as the incarnation of divine love cancels the appropriateness of capital punishment in the New Testament era has little to commend it. Some have appealed to love to justify divorce and thus weaken the principle of monogamous marriage, even as they appeal to love to cancel the mandate for capital punishment. But neighbor-love and social justice are best preserved by a regard for a marital commitment to monogamy and an awareness that the taking of human life is an offense to God. Jesus upholds the high view of the value of human life and of the permanence of monogamous marriage.

I am not much impressed by appeals to the account of the dismissal of the woman taken in adultery in John 8 in order to discount capital punishment. For one thing, the passage does not appear in the earliest and best manuscripts. But even if it is a reliable tradition, as it well may be, the account teaches something else. The prevalent situation was that in cases of adultery the woman was routinely punished while the male participant went scot-free. Jesus invited those who were "without sin" to cast the first stone. In any case, the passage cannot be used to depict Jesus as hostile to capital punishment.

Jesus reminded Pilate that implementation of the death penalty is a divinely entrusted responsibility to be fulfilled justly (John 19:11). He warned Peter that to "die by the sword" is the punishment proper to those who take human life (Matt. 26:52); it should be noted that the sword was meant for execution, not for life imprisonment. Paul indicates that capital punishment was a prerogative divinely conferred on civil government (Rom. 13:14), and in Acts 25:11 he indicates that he would submit to a death sentence if he were "an offender worthy of death."

But even the Old Testament requires high caution in imposing a death sentence as seen in its requirement of several confirming witnesses. Only in cases of deliberate, premeditated murder is it enforced; it is not imposed for the taking of a life without premeditation under the impulse of a crisis situation or as a consequence of negligence (homicide) or gross carelessness (manslaughter) in which the death is involuntary and inadvertent. But in cases of intentional murder, injustice already done to the victim is compounded by further injustice except by the death of the murderer.

Mankind's duty of rendering life for life is not to be carried out in a context of private vengeance, but rather in a context of civil government which under God wields the power of life and death. Where the state considers the life of a deliberate murderer to have greater value than the life of an innocent victim, it demeans the *image Dei* in mankind and weakens the supports of social justice.

We do not, to be sure, live in a theocracy, as when God dictated the Hebrew law of the land. But the social commandments of the law nonetheless remain ideally normative for a stable society and for civil government, whether in ancient pagan Rome or in modern secular America. Paul instructs Christians in Rome not to fear the ruler's power but to merit his praise by the practice of love that eschews murder, adultery, theft, false witness and coveting. Modern nations—bureaucratic, democratic, or chaotic—determine their own destiny. Disregard of the revelatory basis and divine answerability of civil law has bred a crisis of crime, a crisis of justice, a crisis of law, a crisis of culture. But the book of Revelation climaxes in a crescendo in which God who gave the moral law calls nations that mollify it to a final judgment. Nowhere does the Bible repudiate capital punishment for premeditated murder; not only is the death penalty for deliberate killing of a fellow-human permitted, but it is approved and encouraged, and for any government that attaches at least as much value to the life of an innocent victim as to a deliberate murderer, it is ethically imperative.

Social justice demands uniform standards of sentencing so that neither race nor economic status will affect the imposition or nonimposition of the death penalty, and moreover requires that the most repulsive criminal's rights be preserved, including humane treatment on death row and retrial if new evidence appears. In all these matters a vigorous social conscience will need to identify itself with the humane treatment of prisoners, including those who have defamed the divine image of their victims.

Yet to offer a convicted murderer a choice of the way in which he prefers to die, commendable as that may be, is to extend to the murderer a privilege that he withheld from the victim; the deliberate murderer acts out of arbitrary assault, against which the law of the state protects even him in its administration of justice.

Justice is warped by an excessive sympathy toward some criminals simply because they are from minorities. Only a skewed sense of justice can dignify crimes as a legitimate form of social protest and view criminals as champions of social justice in a society that is declared to be intrinsically unjust. Part of the penalty some social critics now pay for their enthronement of sentiment over discernment is that they can scarcely tell right from wrong.

The rejection of capital punishment is not to be dignified as a "higher Christian way" that enthrones the ethics of Jesus; it rather reflects a sub-Christian view that discloses the pervasive penetration of neo-pagan thinking.

WHERE WILL EVANGELICALS CAST THEIR LOT?

Six years ago Jerry Falwell surprised the religious right when he pleaded openly for a new evangelical-fundamentalist alliance. In *The Fundamentalist Phenomenon* (Doubleday, 1981) Falwell held out hope that all conservative Christians might unite in a nationwide cooperative thrust. His projection seems now to have been stillborn, despite the fact that the evangelical magazine *Christianity Today* gave it full play.

Nonetheless, the American evangelical movement today, encamped between fundamentalism on the right and ecumenism on the left, appears more vulnerable to realignment than for a generation.

For better or worse, diversification has increasingly become the hallmark of evangelicalism. Some observers consider this a sign of maturity, others a sign of instability. Some detect an unprecedented opportunity to outflank the movement, or at least to deploy it into new channels, thus altering and perhaps reversing goals for which it was launched early in the 1940s.

Falwell's plea is now overshadowed by another proposal, this time from the evangelical left, more particularly from within the ecumenical movement. Its goal is an evangelical-ecumenical alliance. In *The Evangelical Movement: Growth, Impact, Controversy and Dialogue* (Augsburg, 1988), Mark Ellingsen of the Institute for Ecumenical Research in Strasbourg, France, takes an outside look at recent fundamentalist-evangelical tensions and prods conservative Christians to unite with interchurch agencies and shape a rejuvenated ecumenism.

A builder of bridges between evangelical ecumenists and independent evangelicals, Ellingsen assesses the evangelical movement

73

in its larger Euro-American context. He thinks that a major ecu-
menical-evangelical dialogue is imminent.

Come what may of the looming ecumenical initiative, it is
clear that little has come of Falwell's plea that evangelicals and
fundamentalists probe a cooperative assault against secular forces
that currently shape American society. In *The Fundamentalist
Phenomenon,* Falwell editorially approved a proposal actually
brainstormed by two able young fundamentalist intellectuals, Ed
Dobson and Ed Hindson, who reflect the increasingly open spirit
of a young fundamentalist vanguard.

But Falwell's projection of an informal fundamentalist-evangelical alliance aroused the hostility of right-wing publications like
Sword of the Lord and of hard-nosed religious rightists like Bob
Jones. The extreme right was not about to moderate its criticism
of Billy Graham's inclusivist crusades, of the National Association
of Evangelicals, and of "neo-evangelicals" whose churches are
ecumenically affiliated. Fundamentalist vitality stems from the
vocal leadership of independent pastors rather than from a cohesive movement; so extremists more readily dictate its direction.

The growing evangelical confusion over Biblical inerrancy, the
National Association of Evangelicals' eager inclusion of diverse
denominations ranging from Calvinists to Pentecostals, and the
differing approaches to social ethics accommodating the emergence of an evangelical left encouraged many fundamentalists to
view evangelicals with disdain.

ANOTHER GREAT COMMUNICATOR

Falwell's rise to media prominence as an electronic evangelist,
and his establishment almost *ex nihilo* of what has become Liberty University, gave evidence that he outran and outthought many
of his fundamentalist colleagues. He sensed that fundamentalism
had lost cognitive credibility, and he aimed to restore it. Fundamentalists had already taken the lead in establishing Christian day
schools and nurtured some of the nation's largest Sunday schools
at a time when Sunday schools and prayer meetings were languish-
ing in broader evangelical circles. Falwell launched the *Fundamentalist Journal* which, as a somewhat biased house organ that shuns
emphasis on fundamentalist-evangelical commonalities, rivals
N.A.E.'s *Evangelical Action.*

Falwell needed but failed to get the evangelical movement's support for his American political crusade launched in the name of the religious right. Although not a few evangelicals shared many of Falwell's views, as the Rev. Walt Tomme of Washington's Capitol Hill Metropolitan Baptist Church says, they resisted what seemed "primarily a political agenda for linkage." Others were skeptical of the radical right's effort to Christianize American politics, while it rejected the ecumenical left's social activism as un-Biblical. Moreover, Falwell's opportunistic fund-raising that focused on issues holding momentary promise of financial return, his exaggerated numerical claims for Moral Majority, his off-the-cuff media "bromides," and the ambiguous relationship between Moral Majority and Liberty Foundation multiplied evangelical fears that Falwell was still very much a fundamentalist at heart. He boasted that fundamentalists had hijacked the evangelical jumbo-jet. Evangelicals meanwhile decided not to travel on the road of public political confrontation. Given a Democratic Congress, moreover, and at least the possibility of a Democratic President after the Reagan era, the political impact of the religious right might soon revert to where it was in 1980.

If Falwell believed in the broader alliance projected by Dobson and Hindson, and shared by associates like Cal Thomas and Nelson Keener, he did not energetically act on that vision. Little changed within fundamentalist ranks generally. Only a few fundamentalist evangelists—most notably Jack Van Impe—broke out of judgmental containment and reached for larger evangelically-identified ministries.

Was Falwell welcoming evangelical cooperation, some asked, not because of commitment to a larger vision but rather for whatever ideological and financial support this might bring to his program of national political engagement? Some of Falwell's associates—including Keener and Thomas—left the fold as too narrowly exclusive; others are ready to do so. They sense that the flank of secular humanism cannot be turned without a penetrating social movement, and that fundamentalism alone—as a network of independent stars—was more positioned to function as a political nuisance, or at best a moderating force, than to achieve a significant cultural breakthrough.

The evangelical movement has problems enough of its own, but at least it was a movement, even if its cohesiveness was increasingly under strain. There is, in fact, much to hearten the evangelical mainstream: the continued visibility and impact of Billy Graham crusades; the multiplication and growth of conservative churches; the missionary umbrella of the Evangelical Foreign Mission Association and of the Independent Foreign Mission Association with a combined world outreach of eighteen thousand. The National Association of Evangelicals' effective Washington office is preoccupied with long-term service issues affecting all conservative churches, not with fund-raising single issues. The Association's World Relief Commission has become the nation's third largest placement agency for refugees. And the N.A.E. headquarters building—located in Wheaton, Illinois (the "Evangelical Jerusalem")—links forty-six thousand churches in seventy-nine denominations and claims a service constituency of many millions of Protestant conservatives. Even if the National Religious Broadcasters has eclipsed the N.A.E.'s annual convention as the annual evangelical media event, the organization has advanced far beyond polemics to promote at least a few long-range goals.

For all that, not all is well with the evangelical movement. Even when *Newsweek* wrote in 1976 of "the day of the evangelical" and of some fifty million Americans who profess to be "born again," that magazine noted some looming incendiary flash points: the debate over Scriptural inerrancy, the suspended verdict on charismatic theology, the controversy over evangelism and social action, and disagreement even on evangelical campuses over socialism and a market economy. *Newsweek* might have mentioned also the lack of a worshipful atmosphere in standard evangelical churches that propels numbers of young evangelicals into the Episcopal Church.

What Ecumenism Can Learn

Ellingsen is not interested simply in luring the evangelical left and middle into open ecumenical identification, but enlists them rather for the sake of encouraging change within his own movement. Ecumenism needs to be sprung loose from a relativistic hermeneutic, he asserts; it sadly lacks any "objective and infallible standpoint." A firm challenge needs to be posed to post-Kantian presuppositions that govern much ecumenical interpretation of Scripture. Evangelicals can insist, moreover, that the ecumenical movement make evangelism, not world unity, its first priority.

The religious "mainline" (as the ecumenical arena prefers to designate itself) has still more to learn from the evangelical movement, Ellingsen states. Evangelical churches are dynamically alive and evangelistically active. Many of their core beliefs are more widely shared by Americans generally than are ecumenical alternatives, so that they have become a powerful and socially acceptable religio-political force. Evangelical schools, moreover, enforce academic requirements with more seriousness than many denominational colleges. Furthermore, ecumenism can learn from evangelicals how to use the mass media effectively; the electronic church has achieved a remarkable following despite its exaggeration of audience statistics, and the C.B.N. network in any case has been a dramatic success.

The liberal ecumenical bureaucracy, Ellingsen says, has lost credibility. Evangelicals can reinforce the scanty belief-structure of mainline churches, can import Biblical missionary vitalities to reverse a declining membership, and can challenge bureaucratic manager-types interested only in sociopolitical change and who are disdainful of evangelicals as unsophisticated adversaries. Evangelicals can revitalize the call to personal Christian commitment and lifestyle. But overriding all else, they should be heard, Ellingsen adds, for their challenge to an experience-oriented theology and for their emphasis on objective Scripture as Word of God and their insistence that differences with Rome over *sola scriptura* be taken seriously.

Speaking for conservative ecumenists, Ellingsen contends that the evangelical-ecumenical separation is not primarily doctrinal; rather, he claims, an ecclesiastical backlash accounts for their separate identity. Although hostile to pluralistic theology, evangelicals accept a remarkable span of theological diversity in their own ranks. They have long opposed the social gospel, but now have a social thrust of their own championed by spokesmen like Orlando Costas, Ron Sider, and René Padilla who are not wholly unsympathetic to liberation theology.

More than that, although evangelicals have long criticized ecumenism's ambiguous view of the Bible, their seminary and college faculties entertain notable differences concerning the nature of Biblical authority, inspiration, and inerrancy. Ellingsen therefore prefers to speak of evangelicals as committed to the "full authority" and "perhaps" to the inerrancy of Scripture.

Ellingsen notes that *The Fundamentals,* influential in the convergence of fundamentalists in the early twentieth century, were already marked by latitude in respect to the Bible, since contributors like James Orr (the Glasgow apologist) held moderately critical views. Within the present-day evangelical establishment, Ellingsen comments, holiness churches tend to a looser view of the Bible than do most fundamentalists and evangelicals, and some charismatics emphasize the Holy Spirit to the neglect of the Bible.

All these signs of tolerance Ellingsen considers a major asset for aggressive evangelical-ecumenical dialogue. While he debunks ecumenical caricature of evangelicals as anti-intellectual devotees of a theology reflective of Southern religiosity, he tends to define evangelical essentials more broadly than evangelicals do. He considers the N.A.E. and *Christianity Today* to be rooted in fundamentalism and disproportionately limelights the evangelical left flank. European evangelicals, says Ellingsen, are much more open to the fallibility of Scripture, and many Third World evangelicals deemphasize inerrancy, or limit it to faith and morals, or more ambiguously, to "God's Word."

Ellingsen's repeated reference to "conservative" evangelicals contributes a sense of equal legitimacy to claims by so-called "liberal evangelicals" to speak authentically also for evangelicalism. Ellingsen notes that some churches not N.A.E.-affiliated already cooperate with both N.A.E. and the National Council of Churches. The Southern Baptist bureaucracy has enlarging N.C.C. relationships, while some leaders shun contacts with the N.A.E.

At this stage, Ellingsen contends, only theological dialogue can resolve these differences. He concedes that erstwhile Catholic-evangelical, Lutheran-evangelical, and Catholic-Pentecostal dialogues have had mixed results. Even if a major evangelical-ecumenical dialogue did not immediately transcend a multiplicity of bilateral dialogues, Ellingsen thinks that the Lutheran priority for justification by grace through faith attaches special promise to Lutheran-evangelical-ecumenical dialogue.

EVANGELICALS ARE ALREADY ECUMENICAL

Evangelical theologians differ, Ellingsen notes, over the propriety of natural theology and the precise relationship between reason and revelation, over theistic evolution and scientific creationism, over the ordination of women to a pastor role, and so on, until a thousand qualifications jeopardize the notion of a uniform evangelical theology. He specifically notes the theological thinness of much of the electronic church with its experiential rather than doctrinal orientation.

Similar criticisms of the evangelical movement—with its eager claim of thirty to fifty million like-minded "born again" Americans—have been made by Reformed evangelicals (who explore a more doctrinally sturdy alternative), by Wesleyan evangelicals (who see Arminian theology obscured in an evangelical potpourri), and by some Pentecostalists (who propose to rescue charismatic experience from theological simplicity). But these groups all cope with many theological disagreements within their own ranks. Almost every denomination today reflects an incomplete doctrinal consensus. Moreover, the lingering influence of neo-orthodoxy on some professedly evangelical seminary campuses (including Southern Baptist schools and Fuller Seminary) and of Marxist social analysis by left-wing evangelicals adds to the confusion, which evangelical magazines do little to dispel when they confer equal visibility on diverse views without giving guidance to readers.

In this relativizing of doctrine Ellingsen sees a high prospect for interfaith dialogue and a hopeful sign of convergence that would overcome almost a half-century of ecclesiastical disaffection. Evangelical Christians are pathetically weak in respect to a shared doctrine of the church, he notes, and this weakness nurtures an openness to a larger ecumenism that offers an overall ecclesiastical canopy of sorts. Moreover, some of the denominations are undoubtedly rooted as much in personality or sociological differences as in doctrinal disputes. Some younger evangelicals exhibit a growing yen for visible church unity; a few are thereby open even to Rome, despite the tumult in contemporary Catholicism.

In any case, Ellingsen believes that evangelical independency is held together by missionary coalitions, parachurch agencies, educational institutions (Bible schools, colleges, seminaries) and by evangelistic programs, more than by churches supplying ecclesiastical cohesion. An extension of the parachurch principle (in distinction from a superchurch goal), Ellingsen suggests, could lead to an ecumenical fellowship that exchanges the demand for detailed doctrinal agreement for a recognition that "theological diversity enriches." How one can be enriched by simultaneously holding that the Pope is Christ's vicegerent and that he is Antichrist, as competing church symbols maintain, he does not explain.

Ellingsen is aware that most evangelicals consider the uncompromised authority—indeed, the inerrancy—of Scripture the theological watershed. The issue of Scripture is always near at hand when he discusses evangelical distinctives. But Ellingsen notes that leading evangelical schools no longer speak with one voice on the matter; even the N.A.E. has some diversity in its own ranks. A "vast majority" of evangelicals doubtless insist on inerrancy—but do so "in different degrees." Some insist only on full Scriptural authority, and some emphasize instead the supreme authority of Christ. Ellingsen holds that "the diversity of approaches to inerrancy" seems to "challenge the unity of the Evangelical Movement so severely as to raise questions about whether one can really identify Evangelicalism as a distinct group of Christians."

Ellingsen discerns a shift even on leading evangelical campuses that moderates their differences from ecumenically-oriented schools. Standards of conduct are less stringent, chapel attendance has become optional, there is larger theological openness among faculty, and not least of all, there is some accommodation of diverse views of Scripture.

VULNERABLE TO ACCOMMODATION?

Will evangelicals concede that some of their divisions are not based on Scripture, but rather on tradition? Can evangelicals square their multitudinous diversities with their profession of the inerrant authority of Scripture, a dilemma all the more problematic when Biblical authority itself has become engulfed by dispute? Are the grounds of evangelical unity too dependent on "disavowals," too affirmatively slim, too lacking in doctrinal depth, to protect evangelicals from larger agreement with ecumenical agencies that view the ecumenical complex itself as God's ecclesial action, where church tradition often serves as a guide, and where a powerful hierarchy coexists with the affirmation of the universal priesthood of believers? Amid its present internal differences, has the evangelical establishment prepared its own constituency for a dialogue that might focus on evangelical disagreement even on issues that the Church in earlier centuries considered theologically important? Might the evangelical movement be open or vulnerable to the accommodation of larger ecumenical diversity provided that this is prefaced by a minimal transconfessional credal statement?

Any assessment that hedges the centrality of Biblical authority mislocates the crucial issue that divides evangelicals and ecumenists. Ellingsen concedes that the emphasis on Scriptural inerrancy with a literal precisionist biblicism is a barrier to ecumenical progress. But he stresses that some influential evangelicals now compromise this, and he thinks a new theory of Biblical interpretation might outflank it.

Ellingsen looks expectantly to narrative (Hans Frei) and to canonical (Brevard Childs) hermeneutics to bridge the evangelical-ecumenical gap and to replace the "old model of biblical inerrancy." Seminaries as diverse as Fuller and Northern Baptist already reflect interest in such alternatives, despite the weaknesses of these theories in respect to historical referentiality and to the propositional revelatory authority of Scripture. Childs establishes the final authority of the canonical text at the expense of the decisive authority of the prophetic-apostolic writings.

The evangelical left, which has largely broken with Biblical inerrancy and holds critical views of Scripture, seems eager for rapprochement with ecumenical forces, although some theological differences distinguish its approach to Scriptural authority and interpretation. The left is nonetheless tempted to give sociopolitical action priority over evangelism and tends to promote "justice-concerns" to the forefront of the religious agenda. The ecumenical movement welcomes the evangelical left not for its remnants of conservative theology as much as for its political radicalism. In the past two decades, the evangelical left provided a sort of theological legitimacy for the ecumenical political agenda by professing to find a Christian basis for violent social change in the Hebrew Exodus, and by presuming to find a basis for Socialist economics in the Old Testament theocracy and in the ministry of Jesus. Ecumenists now hope that evangelical moderates will breathe new life into the lagging quest for organizational unity.

Although Ellingsen makes much of evangelical theological diversity (especially the existing differences over Scripture), he fails to stress that evangelicals are united by a much larger bond of commonalities than are ecumenicals, and that the range of ecumenical theological conflict is far more distressing. Evangelical differences do not erode a common core of beliefs; a basic theological consensus survives, even if its struts are not as firm as they might be. The warrant remains the self-revealing God and Christ's gospel authorized by inspired Scripture. A creational and christocentric message is secure.

Many theological differences that Ellingsen finds among evangelicals actually predate the present-day evangelical movement by centuries, and belong to the long history of doctrine or to conflict even in the Reformation and post-Reformation churches. Not only these same divergences, but many more as well, exist within the ecumenical movement. One might by extension of Ellingsen's argument plead the case for a return to Rome rather than a pilgrimage to Geneva.

Ecumenism is an objectionable alternative rather than a glittering attraction, in the eyes of many evangelicals, because of evangelicalism's clear limits to doctrinal tolerances; ecumenical pluralism can and has embraced Unitarians, Swedenborgians, and even nontheists. Evangelicals contend that ecumenism perverted the gospel despite its affirmation of "a common witness" beneath theological differences. For all Ellingsen's complaint over a lack of confessional interest among independent evangelicals and his commendation of the confessional orientation of ecumenically-affiliated denominations, the conceptual weakness of ecumenical doctrine and its erosion of the force of the ancient creeds through theological pluralism is all too evident.

Ellingsen notes that the charismatic movement, which aims to infiltrate all denominations, already supplements the evangelical base in the ecumenical arena, and that ecumenical denominations have increasingly looked to Inter-Varsity/Urbana for missionary recruits, and to Fuller Theological Seminary for ministerial candidates. But if a sturdy evangelical component presently exists in the ecumenical movement, many independent evangelicals ask, why has it counted for so little in the determination of ecumenical policy? Can the leopard, they ask, change its spots? Is there any well-founded reason to think that the insistent ecumenical donning of revolutionary causes, the resignation to a radically pluralistic theology, the openness to salvific universalism, and the hostility to an objectively authoritative Bible can now really be reversed? Many evangelicals contend that the failure of evangelicals inside the ecumenical movement to achieve any substantial alteration of the ecumenical agenda—its radical political commitments, its devaluation of evangelism, and its conflict over the very concepts of divine revelation and Biblical authority—shows that neo-Protestant ecumenism is on an irreversible course. Neo-Protestant ecumenism, they believe, is more likely to welcome liaison with American Catholicism than with historic evangelicalism. The more Ellingsen stresses that evangelicals already significantly participate in ecumenism as a high minority, the more he raises questions about why they have not been able to achieve a significantly conservative leadership and policy. If Luther could not reform Rome, can evangelicals realistically expect to reform the National Council of Churches or the World Council of Churches?

Yet the questions remain whether in their present alignments and subdivisions evangelicals actually provide a vigorous theological and cultural climate, whether they offer powerfully constructive alternatives amid the civilizational crisis, whether they speak pointedly to the mind and conscience and will of modernity, and whether—should Western civilization continue its decline to raw paganism—evangelicals can be counted on to live cohesively as the new society that carries within itself the spiritual and moral fortunes of humanity.

Local churches more and more frequently regard ecumenical rivalries as diversionary. Critical of the cultural *status quo,* they purpose to become community fellowships alert to the risen and returning Christ and seek personal transformation on the way to public impact for truth, justice, and grace. They sense that townspeople will recognize the living Lord's disciples once prayer meetings are again filled, once offenders repent and make restitution, once believers manifest a joy in living that escapes their world-steeped neighbors, once those neighbors are loved as "family." These churches are impatient with disputations over a "pure church"; what they want instead is spiritual and moral vitality born of saturation in the Bible and thus reinforced against world-wickedness. They realize that no fellowship can long countenance neutrality amid cosmic evil without costly consequences; they want both internally and externally to be on the move with Christ only, Savior and Lord. Perhaps on that perspective is where evangelicals had best pin their hopes; for starters at least, that agenda has the ring of apostolic authenticity.

PART FOUR:

EDUCATION AND THE QUEST FOR TRUTH

ELEVEN

FACING THE CRISIS IN EDUCATION

Not for many decades has education been the target, as it currently is, of such deep scrutiny and criticism. Not only teaching methods but also the very content of formal learning, and even its value, is presently under attack. Can we project an evangelical agenda?

1. Parental responsibility for shaping the ideas and ideals of the oncoming generation has priority. The imperative of training a child to walk morally and spiritually (Prov. 22:6) does not, of course, reduce to "throwing the Book" at the younger generation. The example of time spent in prayer, worship, Bible study and church participation, the reading of quality books and magazines, the nature of social life, the way the family makes crucial decisions, and not least of all open conversation and discussion of cardinal ethical and religious concerns define the character of home life.

2. The church has responsibility for perpetuating the Christian heritage. It must not seek to transfer this duty to civil government. The church is not primarily a building that posts hours of public access; it is an assembly or fellowship of believers. Popular education was motivated originally by the church's conviction that a body of information—good news—must be shared with every living man, woman, and child. If the churches are doctrinally weak and experientially oriented, they will obscure the cognitive content and supports of revelatory truth.

3. Christianity insists that revealed truth is universally normative and is not merely perspectival. By contrast, the defection of much public education from theism and the governing influence of atheistic humanism tend to relativize all truth claims, to promote skepticism over the supernatural, and to antiquate evangeli-

cal credal commitments. Christian education cannot afford merely to circumvent the naturalistic option by escapist alternatives that do not engage the crisis of contemporary civilization as a life-or-death matter. Evangelical scholarship must not only maintain a stake in public learning, but it must also illumine the control issues in the context of intellectual history from a theistic vis-a-vis naturalistic perspective. Efforts of the Institute for Advanced Christian Studies and of the Society of Christian Philosophers are contributing to this end, as are evangelical scholars teaching in the secular arena. Parachurch student movements have functioned on the edge of classroom learning to preserve and commend a theistic commitment. But deep penetration of secular education remains an unfulfilled task.

4. Evangelical schools—from kindergarten through college—have been promoted both as principially necessary to present a cohesive world-life view and as strategically necessary to avoid losses to humanistically-loaded instruction. These institutions have channeled much notable evangelical leadership into modern society. Yet of some thirteen million American university and college students, less than ninety thousand are enrolled on campuses represented in the Christian College Coalition. Some of these campuses, moreover, too much take the secular institutions as a model, and critics ask whether concessions to alien views may not impair their effectiveness in conveying a cohesive Christian perspective (cf. J. D. Hunter, *Evangelicalism*, University of Chicago Press, 1987). The Coalition has recently adopted as its motto "For Enduring Values" at a time when public education is struggling to rise above ethical relativity and mere value-clarification. More than fifty years ago, when secular universities forsook God as the integrating factor in learning, they turned instead to "shared" values—only to discover that values divorced from metaphysical anchorage cannot escape a relativizing fate. Moreover, in *The Closing of the American Mind* (Simon and Schuster, 1987), Allan Bloom criticizes the modern displacement of absolutes by values. In the conflict between Biblical theism and naturalism, evangelicals need most of all to vindicate the intellectual credibility of theism and to exhibit the cognitive weaknesses of humanism and raw naturalism, rather than to rely on untenable theories of natural morality.

5. Evangelical Christians need a deepened commitment to higher education and a probing of new pilot projects to penetrate

secular liberal arts learning. Just as various student movements like Inter-Varsity, Campus Crusade, Navigators and others should not be viewed competitively because of different approaches, so diverse experimental research and classroom efforts should be encouraged to bridge to the secular arena. Tyndale House near Cambridge University could well supply a model for similar American efforts. C. S. Lewis College is being projected as an effort by qualified conservative Protestant and Catholic scholars who for two years would on the edge of a secular university teach the Great Books in the context of the Greatest Book, after which students would in two more years complete work for a standard degree issued by the adjacent university. Many students question the worth of university learning which for $20,000 to $40,000 equips them mostly with knowledge of space-time relativities that need to be perpetually updated but leaves graduates without moral absolutes.

6. The evangelical colleges would do well to look anew at their curriculums and ask how best to enhance the excitement of serious learning in the present culture context. Some are tempted to inject an activist dimension by involving students in social and political enterprises for academic credit. Some courses no doubt benefit from practical requirements, and instructors and parents are delighted in a drug-and-sex society to see collegians constructively engaged. But when such activism competes with time for serious study, and when the excitement of learning is shifted from the classroom to external activities, we need to remind ourselves that the world of ideas is the primary focus of an institution of learning that presumably functions as the intellectually critical center of culture. Without clear understanding of the Christian world-life view and a cohesive philosophy, evangelical activism will through its diversity and conflict nullify its own social impact. Somewhere an evangelical college may rise to the challenge of our culture by enrolling incoming freshmen in a course on Plato's *Republic* and on the great motifs of the Bible, and by sending seniors into our decadent society with a lucid comprehension of the Christian world-life view.

TWELVE

EDUCATING FOR INTELLECTUAL EXCELLENCE

How shall we best advance the excitement of serious learning, asks my correspondent, in the present culture context?

That serious learning needs to be promoted few of us will question; to neglect it is an invitation to unenlightenment and inerudition.

The content of ideal education may, to be sure, be in deep dispute: what the classroom sometimes energetically champions may do more harm than good. But ideas, for all that, are gravely important. Not to be fortified with good ideas is to be victimized by bad ones. For, as we are now often reminded, "ideas have consequences."

Yet other prongs of this question—concerning classroom excitement and contemporary culture—call for a closer look. The classroom can surely get along best without some kinds of excitement. Students have assaulted teachers, pulled switchblades, and otherwise intimidated them. Teachers have resorted to gadgetry and gimmickry, and a few exhausted instructors have told offending students to go to Gehenna. In the aftermath of the AIDS crisis, moreover, nothing seems to stimulate student interest more than sex education about condoms. The classroom might well take a critical look at the combustible climate of current learning and ask what atmosphere is most conducive to serious study. Not every form of excitement contributes to excellence in education. The melodramatic is more appropriate to theatrical studies than to the liberal arts.

The bearing of contemporary culture likewise deserves some comment. It is crucially important that teachers and students recognize it for what it is, grasp its controlling beliefs and behavior-patterns, and do full justice to its intentions. Education taught in a cultural vacuum short-changes the student who must live his life, as we do, in a particular historical context and must understand its far-reaching implications. We are not contemporaries of Plato or of Paul or of Hegel but of Stephen J. Gould and Carl Sagan who despise the supernatural and, even more, seem wholly ignorant of divine commandments and of revealed truths. No teacher does serious learning any service who implies the finality of contemporary culture and represents its conceptual content as the acme of truth and the criterion of wisdom. Modern culture is the expression of one particular epoch in the much longer chain of human history, and it has no authentic basis for claiming ultimacy for its representations of reality, truth and good.

The desirable excitement of serious learning begins, therefore, with a studied look at presuppositions that even educators often take for granted: such as that spine-tingling classroom confrontation is all to the good, that relatedness to contemporary culture necessarily serves the student well, and so on. Here we already enter the arena of disputable ideas whose differing implications, often covert, shadow all of life.

Someone will surely ask whether ours is not an activistic age, an era impatient with concepts and clamoring instead for social involvement. Should not the excitement of learning be advanced by mobilizing the classroom for community action? Does not Christian education, aware that the New Testament requires us to "*do* the truth" (and not simply to learn or know it), demand that concept and comportment stay together like husband and wife? Has not Christian learning been too much dominated by the classic Greek view that whoever knows the truth will do it? In brief, should we not alter classroom requirements so that academic credit requires community or public engagement reflective of evangelical conceptual commitments?

Here we need to distinguish several matters. Surely it is the case that Christianity rejects the notion that whoever knows the truth will do it; Greek philosophers, who were silent about the sinfulness of man, underestimated the role of volition and assumed the divinity of the human mind. And Christian learning must have in view the goal of Christianity in society and shape a philosophy of culture and of politics that articulates the Christian vision of man in society. Education which leaves students without an awareness of those commitments short-changes the younger generation. A distinctive behavior is rightly expected of evangelical students in a campus-community manifestation of basic beliefs. Some college classes may properly involve larger public engagement as a legitimate part of course study for credit—in education, practice teaching; in political science, local precinct activity; in social science, community service. Yet any notion that the excitement of the classroom is best preserved by shifting the focus from the clash of ideas to public activism is misguided; community involvement on the wrong premises can do more harm than good to student and society alike.

The conflict of ideas and their resolution in the classroom remains the critical center of serious learning. Not doing the truth will condemn us, but not knowing it—when in fact earnest education can uncover it—is worse still, since it dooms us to doing the right thing only by chance, if at all. Intellectually unanchored experience is like a yacht unpredictably tossed about on the high seas and outside the final authority of any country. The college or university is the intellectually critical axis of society, and if the Christian takes seriously his citizenship in two worlds he dare not be disengaged from either.

What this requires is philosophically-sensitive teachers and students, alert both to personal and to cosmic concerns and to pursuing world-life perspective. The task is the more complex today because, much as secular humanism remains the covert conceptuality of much liberal arts learning, contemporary American society is now sundered by a plurality of cultures and a widening diversity of worldviews. Education increasingly faces the burden of wrestling these conflicting and competing currents and of unmasking their divergent depictions of the real world and of the human predicament and its resolution. They define the problem of evil and the meaning of the good in rival ways, and variously explain the struggle against hostile powers.

The tug of neo-paganism pulls humanism toward raw naturalism, and shapes an agenda that strikes against evangelicalism and other options as well. Anti-intellectualism yields a ready welcome to new cults, for it does not penetrate to the essential distinction between Judeo-Christian creational transcendence and the immanental spiritism of apparently new but actually archaic religious options.

That is not to say that effective education consists of stuffing

93

an assortment of empty skulls with conceptual data. It differs from teaching elephants and horses to count, even if aided by acrostics and alliteration, or from simply adding "another room" to a sprawling ranch house.

Students do not now come to the classroom mentally unstuffed. If they are rooted in secular modernity they are preloaded with cultural biases acquired from playmates, neighbors, radio and television and cassettes. Much of this information is unorganized, and some of it incapable of organization; most of it offers little in the way of moral and spiritual illumination. God, if included at all, gets a formal nod or merely honorific role; who He really is, and what His objective is, remains a mystery. An astonishing number of students do not rise above the artificial and decadent view of life fostered by the soap operas, and surprisingly few are familiar with great works of literature. Even a television program like "It's Academic," commendable as it is for its motivation of smart students, carries little assurance of intellectual integration of unrelated data, or of life perspective.

The evangelical student comes to college with a considerably different stance. He or she knows refreshingly more about God than his or her secular counterpart. Nevertheless, with some few gratifying exceptions, neither home nor church has shaped a comprehensive and consistent faith that stands noon-bright amid the dim shadows of spiritual rebellion and moral profligacy. Too often such students are tempted to link excitement with the renegade world and find Christian commitment drab. They have not intellectually won the Biblical heritage for themselves but merely parrot it. They are seldom any longer models of ethical purity, for the social climate has tarnished their value-system, and interest in vocational opportunity outruns interest in intellectual power and moral consistency. Personal excitement is focused on inner experience rather than on objective truth—as if the validity of experience can somehow be assured on merely subjective grounds. Theological depth and philosophical power are considered inessential life-support factors.

How does the Christian college penetrate this mood and thrust its students beyond narrow channels of private interest into broad and deep rivers of cognitive concern? Can we get past administrators who are satisfied if education simply helps build character, adds personal life perspective, and enhances vocational objectives? Do not many educators greet with dragging feet any proposal to alter a curriculum hard-won in the face of academic turf battles?

We need to set collegiate learning in the context not simply of contemporary culture but rather in the context of intellectual history, and to put students in touch with the primary sources. We stand upon the shoulders of the past, and in often unwitting ways we think with minds indebted to ancient and medieval as well as modern conceptual networks. Instead of overdependence on secondary sources, students need to be put into direct touch with the influential intellects and the Great Books—not only the works commended by Mortimer Adler but other equally important Christian works also with a focus on God who speaks and acts. The Bible will not be missing on any worthy manifest of monumental literature.

These sources thrust upon the reader the perennially significant questions: *Who* am I? *Why* am I? *Where* am I going? Does human life make sense, and if so what is its meaning? The world asks these questions out of desperation, the Christian in search of confirmation. The Great Books underscore not only the indispensability but also the practicality of these concerns. On the answer hangs the very nature of truth, of the good, and of human worth.

Nor should we simply breast-feed incoming college students until they are ready for reading "the greats"; a student unready to ingest such works should be required to take remedial preparatory courses. The very first course—perhaps a full-time freshman module—might well be Plato's *Republic,* which interacts with materialism from a supernatural stance, deals with the sad break-up of Greek democracy, discusses the ideal content of education, wrestles the nature of truth and the good, and interacts with much else that is also of critical contemporary concern.

The next course might well take the Bible as its basic book in revelatory confrontation of both philosophical idealism and naturalism. An educational program alert to presuppositions and to the importance of logical tests could then well find its climax in a senior required course on Biblical theism and Christian ethics. That comprehensive overview is much more important than majoring only in changing space-time relativities that need constantly to be revised.

The shift from secular to Biblical metaphysics and ethics will inevitably focus on the crown jewel of human history—namely, Jesus Christ the God-man. In Greek philosophy one does not speak of the Plato-centeredness or of the Aristotle-centeredness of classic metaphysics and ethics, but Christianity speaks insistently of the Christ-centeredness of its outlook. What Jesus said and did, and the New Testament ethic predicated on His divine authority, work, and teaching, are definitive and exemplary for the Christian enterprise. Without the centrality of Christ, Christianity is but another speculative cult. The New Testament forces upon the model of the good man the indispensability of faith, hope and love as life-transforming values that undergird spirituality. No less does it connect a soul-integrating stance with godly activity in neighbor and community involvements. Christian commitment is not mere devotion to a revered tradition, but carries a demand for the believer's total response in home and society.

Of course, evangelicals cope today with a tide of debatable hermeneutics that converts the Biblical texts into instruments of political or social change and clothes preferred courses of action with pseudo-textual authority. The cult of revolution-theology is but one example. An important element of theological education is a decision for or against the legitimacy of positions and programs alleged to be grounded in the truth of the text.

In the current largely anti-intellectual climate, which has made substantial inroads not only into evangelical televangelism but also into evangelical academe, one can almost anticipate the tortured groans and complaints of those who insist that not every student intends to be a theologian or philosopher. That is not the point, however. The leaders of the Protestant Reformation were all university-trained, and they knew the Biblical languages and the Bible's content and its implications. In that great turning-time the laity knew more about theology than do many pastors today, armed as they may be with even a Doctor of Ministries degree. Evangelical leaders often speak enthusiastically of the prospect or hope of a new Reformation. If they intend this seriously, they must face up to its educational demands.

There may be other ways of promoting Christian education in depth, but every way of not doing it more effectively seems too shallow to challenge the naturalistic mainstream. When our Christian forefathers founded Harvard and Columbia, they did not have in mind merely salvaging the saints. If independent evangelical colleges do not rise to intellectual confrontation, they should not be surprised if challenging alternatives arise, perhaps shaped by conservative ecumenists and conservative Catholics along with uneasy evangelical independents. Christian education that is not intellectually demanding may be living on borrowed time.

THIRTEEN

CHRISTIAN FUND-RAISING HERESIES

Despite the risk of worshiping it, money—at least some of it— is indispensable. There is nothing evil about fund-raising to establish, preserve and enlarge legitimate Christian enterprises. One task of evangelical institutions is to persuade potential donors that their activities are worthy of generous support.

Nor does modernity force upon evangelical organizations a choice between the spiritual and the technological generation of financial help. When an enterprise depends, as many do, on tens and hundreds of thousands of donors, personal contact is possible with only a limited few, and technology provides the means of continuing access.

Yet there is ever-present danger that fund-raising will encroach upon the spiritual vitality and moral integrity of evangelical enterprises. This is true of educational, of evangelistic and of charitable agencies.

Some administrators are as unlearned about economic matters as they are naive about the use of the media. One college lost valuable property through a seemingly advantageous deal with an all-too-clever shyster. We can understand why most administrators readily enlist professional fund-raisers and investment agencies. Some three hundred thousand planners today offer their services to the public. There are risks galore. In the transfer of financial activities to professional managers, administrators may in fact unwittingly lose control of an institution's destiny. The faculty of an evangelical seminary lost retirement benefits some years ago when a highly touted insurance plan collapsed. One informed evangelical leader volunteered to me that he would not turn over funding operations to more than three or four of the many hundreds of professional fund-raisers. Their performance record, reaching back through at least one Wall Street bear market, is important. No less important is the character of an outside staff that will have intimate access to an institution's financial sources.

Yet the day is virtually gone when evangelical leaders, like George Mueller earlier in this century, mainly trust God's providence and make little public mention of their needs.[1] As budgets spiral ever upward, college trustees seek presidential leadership skilled in public relations and in fund-raising from large foundations. One prominent administrator complained some decades ago because a requisite daily reading of the *Wall Street Journal* parched his soul; it may have worsened his migraine also. Reading the *Journal* is not, of course, administratively off-limits; reports of corporate executives who sell large blocs of their own stock at handsome profits can identify possible future donor sources. But the need to meet large budgets, the sophistication required in preparing grant proposals, the importance of personal contacts in the financial world, all tend to treat God as a Peeping Tom in economic affairs, except when deficits so threaten survival that no earthly hope remains but a return to the prayer meeting.

Not a few enterprises take their promotional cue from Madison Avenue, and eagerly taper their appeals to secular approaches. Some ministries refuse to make public their doctrinal or financial statements and meticulously avoid identification with the Evangelical Council for Financial Accountability. So intense is the evangelical rivalry for dollars that short-term evangelistic projects are sometimes pitted competitively against long-term educational enterprises.

The notion of "heresies" in fund-raising may seem not quite appropriate. Yet fund-raising today does incorporate significant deviations from orthodox methods and policies. Fund-raising techniques and themes once viewed with disdain are becoming as common in evangelical circles as are botanical hairdos and skin-grafted jeans in secular society. We need to address serious questions to some nonconformists and innovators.

Among major controversial issues are whether Christian institutions should actively seek funding from nonevangelical foundations; whether familiar Biblical passages on stewardship can properly be channeled into solicitations for modern parachurch movements; whether even evangelical enterprises may be guilty of "bait-and-switch" tactics; whether a "prosperity theology" is a legitimate means of enlisting donors; whether premium offers, including cheap trinkets depicted as having intrinsic spiritual power, are akin to medieval indulgences; whether so-called "junk mail" can in good conscience be represented as priority personal correspondence.

Unfortunately, evangelical fund-raising practices are sometimes more shoddy than those of nonreligious agencies. Some secular agencies maintain a level of integrity in the use of funding techniques that even religious enterprises may well emulate. Christian organizations of every kind therefore need to evaluate funding practices not only in order to critique the secular milieu, but for their own sakes also, and for the good of the larger evangelical cause.[2]

The growing evangelical pursuit of funds from nonevangelical or secular foundations raises vexing problems. Some administrators are inclined to "take all the Devil's money you can get, and put it to godly uses." Others balk at drafting proposals that deliberately downplay specifically Biblical convictions in order to shape programs that non-Christian philanthropies are most likely to approve. To be sure, there may be overlapping moral and scientific concerns of interest to both evangelical institutions and secular foundations. No objection can be mounted if available funding does not oblige the receiving institution to compromise its own principles and does not encourage reliance on secular sources that in time may deviate an institution from its distinctive commitments.[3] It is not unthinkable that in order to secure outside funding that removes personal financial pressure from themselves trustees may moderate an institution's commitments. An evangelical college must in any event be supremely concerned that nothing shall erode its loyalty to God, its devotion to charter objectives, the goodwill of its constituency, and dependence upon prayer for faithful survival.

The notion that gifts may be advantageously solicited from wealthy persons irrespective of their basic convictions often leads fund-raisers to conform proposals to the special interest of one or another monied prospect. Helen Bergan's *Where the Money Is: A Fund Raiser's Guide to the Rich* (Alexandria, Va., VioGuide Press) then becomes the solicitor's main sourcebook. The *Chicago Tribune*'s biweekly newsletter *Donor Briefing* ($150 a year) alerts him to who is giving what to whom and why. Yet the fund-raiser may be quite unaware that buying into nonevangelical or subevangelical funding may in the long run do as much harm to a ministry's theological and spiritual orientation as it does good to its present fiscal condition. As a compensation for their gifts some large donors have expected personal or proxy representation on a board or governing body.

Fund appeals are almost routinely cloaked with some aura of Biblical legitimation. Malachi 3:8-10 is frequently invoked for "storehouse giving." In view of this passage, many pastors encourage channeling all one's contributions through the local church, whereas others no less energetically promote support of parachurch organizations. Yet complex hermeneutical presuppositions underlie an extension of this passage to any and all modern giving. If we evade sound exegesis and open such texts to allegorical meanings, what are the overall implications for Scripture?

Often an appeal letter will begin with a Bible text (e.g., "Thanks be to God for His unspeakable gift," 2 Cor. 9:15) and, having enlisted Jesus Christ merely as a transitional theme, will then conclude by soliciting funds for some current project and promising each donor the promoter's latest book brimful of unprecedented spiritual blessing. Seldom is the fund-seeker content to mention a need for which he is "looking to the Lord in faith" without the further suggestion that the Lord in turn is looking to the letter's recipient to handle the matter in His absence.

More disconcerting is the notion prevalent in some circles that in fund-solicitation "the end justifies the means." Since the church "does good" in the world, it can merchandize whatever turns a quick dollar to support the cause. Many local churches, although usually not evangelical in identification, resort to house-to-house peddling to support special projects. For more than twenty years some groups have offered items that Revere Company says "sell like magic" and make "eye-popping profits": not Bibles, devotional studies and soul-stretchers but jelly beans, bedtime teddy bears and dish cloths. The saddest aspect of this is that as Resurrection Sunday approaches, the church leaves the impression that Christianity is a matter of going into all the world to peddle Easter-egg dye.

Such examples are by no means the most offensive. Some churches rely on "bingo," raffles and lotteries to stay out of the red. Salesian Missions, which identifies itself with forty thousand Salesian priests, brothers and sisters, recently sent to its large mailing list six sweepstakes tickets on a new Olds Firenza as a lure for $5 contributions to its child-support ministry.

Even the secular press has taken note of the fact that the "bait-and-switch" technique is moving from the world of commercial advertising into churches and synagogues, and into other kinds of ministries. Charles Trueheart, *Washington Post* staff writer, comments on "a growing sophistication by Christian and Jewish congregations at developing 'bait-and-switch' techniques to beef up their flocks—settings for singles to meet mates, for example." When a snow emergency postponed church and school meetings, Baptists in northern Virginia learned from cancellation announcements on television that one of their houses of worship was sponsoring a weekly class in ballroom dancing.

Some evangelists push all the "hot buttons" of human misery in their appeal letters, and then shift attention to alternative ministries for which support is really sought and for which requested funding will actually be used. Appeals sometimes focus on earthquakes, famines and other human crises even when the soliciting organizations lack proper structures for implementing relief programs. Sometimes photos have been mislabeled and composite stories have been depicted as true accounts.

Evangelical agencies frequently seek to impress potential donors by subordinating an institution's main rationale for existence to present activities that differ notably from those for which it was founded. The final 1986 appeal letter of a national evangelical association, for example, speaks not of gains in evangelical affiliation and transevangelical unity as much as the movement's current crusade against pornography, and moreover of its having "educated the IRS in the exemption battle for church auxiliaries." The letter pleads for gifts to launch a "1987 offensive" to complete the victories of 1986 lest the nation "be torn asunder." The nearest hint of transevangelical progress is a somewhat ambiguous statement that the organization "is uniquely able to link 46,000 churches" without indicating that they are still divided into seventy-nine different denominations.

Too much evangelical advertising fails to highlight crucial core beliefs. Even during the 1986 Graham crusade in Washington, D.C., the *Washington Post* carried a large advertisement featuring the evangelist but with no mention of God. Not a few evangelical institutions today use ambiguous terms to gloss over the issue of Biblical reliability.

Most evangelical agencies, though not all, avoid adducing a "prosperity-theology" as a motivation for giving: the more you give, the wealthier you become. Some invoke Luke 6:38 ("Give and it shall be given unto you") as a reciprocity-guarantee, thus obscuring Jesus' teaching cited by the Apostle Paul: "It is more blessed to give than to receive" (Acts 20:35). The spiritual rewards of stewardship are thus subordinated to the supremacy of material blessing. Successful entrepreneurs who stress that God has been instrumental in the growth of their business wittingly or unwittingly reinforce such prosperity-theology. The error of the prosperity theme is not its emphasis that God blesses commercial integrity and sacrificial stewardship, nor that business success is attributable to divine providence, but rather its conversion of stewardship into a material prosperity tool, its attachment of giving to the expectation of personal financial benefit, its correlation of spirituality with material gain. This approach fails to see stewardship first and foremost as a spiritual exercise for the glory of God and the advancement of His goals, one that when the giving is sacrificial yields distinctive compensations of character to the donor.

Sometimes the appeal for "seed faith" or "seed money" is simply a variety of prosperity-theology: funds are solicited with the assurance that God will not only repay the gift materially, but will also multiply the donor's investment. Apart from such distortion, the notion of seed money has much to commend it as a launchpad for pilot projects.

Fund-raising premiums raise more urgent ethical problems. For one thing, the monetary value of such premiums is often exaggerated. At worst, special spiritual worth is attributed to floral sprigs or tiny twigs from the Holy Land, or mother-of-pearl crosses from Bethlehem, or olive wood amulets from Jerusalem, or cheap jade charms from Hong Kong or Taiwan. Such relics may not carry all the implications of medieval indulgences. But they are reminiscent of them nonetheless insofar as they are depicted as laden with blessing, if not with miracle-power, because they have been prayed over or are thought to protect the recipient against evil. If this were merely a religious extension of the cosmetic industry's "free bonus with purchase," it would be bad enough; far worse is the promise not merely of physical enhancement, but of spiritual benefits that the almost worthless trinkets are presumed to convey.

Books, magazines or cassettes are frequently sent as premiums. Donors must deduct their value from any claim for a tax-exempt contribution. The hawker often puts their value not at actual cost but at the publisher's or producer's inflated price. IRS requirements are more murky when gift books are provided by an independent source to help stimulate support for a program. Publishers' closeouts, now and then distributed by evangelical agencies, often do little to enhance organizational goals. Some tax-exempt groups are careful to distribute books that reflect an organization's creative interests and achievements, thereby stimulating larger long-term support. Doctrinally responsible ventures will distribute books of theological integrity that truly promote a spiritual life. "Health and wealth" solicitations are often somewhat more ambiguous than are theologically-articulate ministries and are sometimes less precise about how contributions will be used. Some theologically-indefinite efforts focus constantly on world emergency needs, and alter their appeal goals and even moderate their doctrinal tenets when they shift to new crisis concerns.

Even if evangelical funding appeals are less than ideal, things could be worse. Much secular fund-raising links generosity in making charitable gifts primarily to the tax break such gifts bestow on donors. In 1986 many charities advised U.S. citizens how they could benefit tax-wise by giving before year-end when the new tax law became effective. Wellesley College projected a "tax alert" warning for its donor list that under the new law the cost of giving could rise by as much as 44 percent. The accounting firm of Arthur Anderson & Co. advised nonprofit institutions that opportunity was vanishing for wealthy donors to "get the government to pay as much as one-half the cost of lifetime charitable giving."

Fortunately, evangelical appeals escape the misleading secular offers of "something for nothing." As far as I know, no evangelical college, for example, has yet promoted an alumni lottery offering free tuition for a child or grandchild, or offering the second-prize winner an all-expense-paid invitation to homecoming weekend for a class reunion. I hesitate to project additional options lest some venturesome promoter be tempted to actualize the possibilities.

Yet many evangelical organizations, and even some Christian colleges, do not wholly escape the temptation to post fake mailgrams or to dress up junk mail to look like first-class personal correspondence. Evangelistic enterprises and humanitarian agencies routinely imprint their envelopes with "Urgent—Immediate Reply Requested" or "Priority Mail" so that gullible recipients may think the correspondence is selective and private.

A more blatantly offensive device is the first-class letter sent by a stranger who addresses the prospect by first name and signs off on a first-name basis. The correspondence shares supposedly confidential information (usually so intangible that its release could harm no one) and charts new evangelistic opportunities that promise certain success. Sometimes this approach takes the form of a Christmas greeting. I usually ask my wife if she knows the writer before the letter vanishes with other junk mail.

A special public relations feature of evangelical education is its vaunted personal interest in the individual student as a person uniquely fashioned in God's image and created for distinctive service in the world. In reality large present-day enrollments and oversized classes, along with heavy faculty demands, continually jeopardize this personal touch, but recollection of earlier college days by alumni often remains a lifelong motivation for dedicated service. Yet smaller colleges, which sometimes boast of a larger one-on-one faculty-student relationship, do not necessarily excel at it. A few years ago, when conducting a faculty survey, I wrote a dozen evangelical colleges for their current catalogue. One institution immediately computerized my name, and for three consecutive years I was invited to enroll as a freshman and to have my parents visit campus at homecoming.

Computer-generated correspondence which gives the impression of a personal exchange is bad enough. But when the mechanical signature guarantees that it will personally pray for all who write expressing their needs—and conveys the impression of a truly significant prayer burden for each respondent—the pitch is unconscionable. One recent solicitation letter from a religious magazine began with the sender's personal assurance that "Today I have your name before me in prayer." One need not major in mathematics to know that even the most determined correspondent would never manage ten thousand three-second sound blips like "O God, remember Carl Henry wherever he is, whatever his need," even if he prayed for eight solid hours without ever stopping for breath (unless of course the prayers were also computerized and names automatically fed into the computerized tape). The writer adds that "I am deeply and strongly on (his) heart" because the American economy may suddenly plummet and seed gifts are needed. The letter proceeds to invert apostolic priorities by saying far more about money than about ministry.

Obviously movements with large supportive constituencies

cannot maintain personal relationships with all donors, and over-statement readily becomes the first step toward manipulating and exploiting the donor base. The temptation also arises, on the basis of an evangelical entrepreneur's private faith, to exceed budget prospects by anticipating support which is not really in hand or in view for new and enlarged ministries. Some such funding appeals have even blamed God for unfortunate overextension of enter-prises: "The Lord has blessed this work so abundantly that now we are really in trouble trying to keep it going." Or again, "With-out additional help we must cut back critical programs, but I know that is not God's will for us."

According to media commentators, "compassion fatigue" fol-lowed the sustained drive carried by established evangelical agen-cies like World Vision and by *ad hoc* relief efforts like Live Aid and Hands Across America to aid countless impoverished multi-tudes in Africa and elsewhere. Yet on the premise that people will not respond to a financially successful effort as readily as to a salvage operation, direct mail experts advise Christian agencies to create a crisis by "pressing the panic button." Conservatively-worded direct mail that deals with substantive issues is said to be financially unrewarding; only by feeding the constituency "raw meat"—homosexuality, pornography, sexual delinquency, drugs, and so on—will the recipient feel sufficiently "moved" to respond.

Financially faltering enterprises may suggest a need for Chris-tian cooperation and merger. Personality-cult movements run great risk when leaders become—as Mel Lorentzen puts it—"builders of personal empires 'in His name' "; rather than serving as "commissioned agents of the heavenly kingdom" they compete with each other for cash from a common constituency. Just as lamentable is the sale and exchange of donor lists by some evan-gelical or fundamentalist agencies. I know that one particular enterprise has bartered my name because I once deliberately mis-spelled it Hhenry; solicitations are now addressed to me that way by at least a dozen sources.

The fact that a cause is good does not of itself justify tele-phone intrusion at any hour of the day or evening. The year-end phonathon is an unpleasant tactic; the caller is not personally known, often interrupts something the responder considers more important, usually solicits a larger contribution than the responder is disposed to make, and demeans the prospect list into a series of technological statistics. How would the president of an offending institution or movement feel if the victims of phonathon lists called him at his home to ask for a contribution to their local churches for community evangelism? Even worse is the long-distance supposedly person-to-person call in which the "operator" asks if one has just a minute to listen to an important personal message from some Big Name Evangelical, and then is subjected to the insult of a recorded tape. I usually hang up; such an approach is an invasion of my time under false pretenses.

Other fund-raisers suggest asking someone from a potential donor's college class or peer group to make the pitch. If the potential donor is personally unable or indisposed to give, fund-raisers then invite the recalcitrant prospect to address the most vulnerable of his well-to-do or wealthy acquaintances. The appeal to donor ego nullifies the ethical and spiritual gratification that donors ought to experience in giving. Another questionable device is that of publishing lists of donors and their gifts, thus making public what ought to be a private matter—namely, the extent of a donor's contribution. This practice exposes contributors to solicitation by still other fund-raisers. Moreover, if such tactics are used to send smaller donors on a "guilt trip," they may alienate an important and perhaps even the largest segment of supporters.

Something more should be said about unworthy pressure techniques upon donors. By any estimate, the decline of Oral Roberts' $500 million evangelical empire is a sad spectacle: closing of the dental school, transfer of the law school, failure of the City of Faith hospital to fill many of its beds, diminution of Oral Roberts University endowment funds, and now a desperate media plea for scholarships that has invited the scorn of Roberts' foes and friends alike. Seeking $4.5 million for medical school scholars, Roberts begged TV viewers to post $100 apiece in quick money lest God take him hostage and doom him to heaven. Media stations in Dallas, Denver, Oklahoma City, Tulsa and Washington rejected the money-begging telecast as unacceptable. At the end of a substitute program, Roberts' son Richard in effect urged viewers to send gifts to spare his father from being taken to heaven. When Roberts reportedly postponed his deadline or lifeline to March 1988, a newspaper columnist speculated that God's credit department must have given Oral a 365-day extension. But whether Oral's D-day is in 1987 or 1988, his appeal discredits a ministry whose overall message has been that sufficient faith can work miracles. It was hardly a gain for the evangelical gospel, moreover, to put the prospect of going to heaven in the category of a calamity. But quite aside from theological concerns, such gimmickry detracts from the financial integrity of evangelical fund-raising.

Evangelical enterprises need constantly to investigate how dependent their promotion is on the philosophy of secular professionals. Madison Avenue's most successful commercials, it is said, are those which stretch the truth but do so subtly. Yet the advertising world was caught off guard recently when a thirty-second television commercial openly caricatured the exaggerated claims of competing car wheelers and dealers. While a smooth huckster ridiculously overstated the virtues of the Japanese Isuzu—top speed of 300 miles an hour and 94 miles a gallon in city driving—the screen carried the background warning: "He's lying!" The huckster continued: "It has more seats than the Astrodome." The Isuzu ad was considered a breakthrough because it openly admitted that usual promotion practices tend to gloss over truth in advertising.

It seems self-discrediting when a college puts itself into the academic major leagues and depicts itself, as did Liberty Baptist College, as the future fundamentalist Harvard even before its campus emerged from the concrete-bunker stage. In any case, Harvard, which even in its divinity school now holds evangelical Christianity at considerable distance, hardly provides the milieu that sound fundamentalism should desire to emulate. (Speaking of insensitive overstatement, I recall that in 1971 an evangelical promoter unblushingly described the Jerusalem Congress on Biblical Prophecy to tour prospects as "the nearest thing to a seat at the Second Coming.").

No less overstated is the designation, by one spokesman, of the Christian College Coalition as a great Christian university of seventy affiliated schools enrolling a total of eighty-five thousand students on related campuses in scores of cities that span the nation. Such comments not only miss the sense of what essentially constitutes a major university, but tend also to dwarf the fact that a vast majority of America's twelve million university students get their learning in nonevangelical schools.

The time has come for full candor in all evangelical promotion. Evangelists who cite impressive statistics of cumulative attendance and of public "decisions" as evidence of success need to play fair with their constituencies and to concede that between 92 and 97 percent of those coming forward at decision-making time do not become active church members. Some promotion has claimed that for ten cents a person all Africa can be evangelized, as if illiteracy and an untranslated Bible are nowhere obstacles in reaching lost and hidden groups.

Even when prospective donors are told that the first $15,000 received would go to meet some dire need, what is often unmentioned is that the first contributions by radio and television audiences usually go toward meeting program and overhead expenses. Unless an independent source has underwritten the salaries of an institution's development or stewardship staff, a substantial part of the money raised goes to pay salaries and travel costs, even where solicitation is done on commission. No fund-raising can be done without administrative costs; few organizations are in a position to devote every cent that is given to the cause for which contributions are intended. Hence the percentage of funds that remains to advance an institution's spiritual and moral vision is crucially important.

Few factors permanently motivate the giving of believers more than a clear, unambiguous definition of objectives enunciated by a leader perceived to be trustworthy. A touch of charisma is an asset, but it will not compensate for a lack of personal integrity or for imprecise formulation of goals or for uncertainty over the intended use of funds. The risk of concentrating the promotion of an enterprise upon a single personality is evident, however; not only does such a policy create problems of succession, but the leader is sometimes also conceived as being more important than the work. Consequently, the temptation arises to perpetuate family dynasties.

Fund solicitation for evangelical enterprises is best done by dedicated believers who are assured of the doctrinal, moral and fiscal integrity of their enterprises and who venture fund-raising primarily as a divine vocation rather than simply for the commission that represents or augments their salaries.

For the Christian educational institution, the issues of fund-raising strategy have a further important implication. In their solicitation of funds, Christian colleges and seminaries may be expected to conduct such efforts as efficiently as any other organization. But no commendation of an evangelical college can surpass that of quality education and the victory for truth it achieves in the struggle for the mind and will of our generation.

Evangelical educational institutions have used the media for fund-raising, but they have not by and large used the media to promulgate Biblical world-life convictions. It is no credit to evangelical educators that television has offered sunrise courses oriented largely to secular humanism, or that educational networks have featured major programs advancing naturalistic evolution; even our most prestigious colleges have done little to invest their educational resources for significant public impact. The fact remains that prominent nonevangelical scholars are invited more frequently as lecturers on evangelical campuses than evangelical scholars on those campuses are invited by faculty at nonevangelical schools to address nonevangelical student audiences. We might well ask why.

As Christianity's critical intellectual center in contemporary society, the evangelical college must take seriously the importance of a learned exposition of the Christian world-life view. The promotional literature of evangelical campuses has for decades rightly oriented their special academic mission to Christian world-life concerns. Yet such literature routinely overstates actual achievement in that realm, for there has often been little more than an elemental exposition of it.

As the cognitive center of the evangelical movement, the Christian campus must place promotion and funding conspicuously in the service of preserving, propagating and vindicating truth. To do this requires an unapologetic statement of doctrinal conviction, a platform of fund-raising principles compatible with those commitments, and a promotional policy that above all else stresses how the institution's faculty and alumni succeed in advancing the triumph of truth in the contemporary world.

No amount of enthusiasm for evangelism, no proposals for expanding or renovating buildings, no plans for increasing faculty salaries, no program of zeal for sports—however proper such interests may be—can compensate for an academic institution's neglect of its proper priority—namely, precision in presenting truth and competence in advancing truth's triumph in today's conflict of ideas. The biggest assets of any evangelical college are its comprehensively integrated Christian world-life view; its instructional and literary contribution of able scholars who expound that view; faculty books and articles that both expose the cognitive weaknesses of modern regnant alternatives and articulate the logical and moral superiority of the Biblical option. Such effort must persevere until adversary thinkers see the need for serious response and evangelical works are widely used not only by Christian college students but also by secular collegians and are accepted as valid parallel reading.

Significant books by evangelical academicians outside the Biblical and theological field have only recently begun to appear, although seldom are such volumes interdisciplinary in nature, except as numerous colleges engage in an exchange of faculty monographs. Evangelical colleges fail their constituencies most of all in respect to Christian world-life view fulfillment. To be sure, all evangelical campuses declare their devotion to it, and feature that devotion as one reason why students should enroll. But faculty delineation is often disappointing, and sometimes barely rises above a devotional level. Surely on an evangelical campus every professor should have some role, however small, in advancing world-life concerns. Secular humanists have gained ascendancy in the realm of liberal learning not because they outnumber evangelical scholars, but in part at least because evangelical scholars seem remote from the cultural clash of ideas and too infrequently and too ineffectively dissect and display the core convictions of contemporary naturalism.

Fund-raising for Christian colleges ideally presupposes institutions that readily proclaim their doctrinal heritage; that have academically gifted faculties devoted to the whole truth and its vindication in the cultural context; that exemplify devotion to the living God in thought and life; that produce alumni who in all their vocational pursuits—from evangelism to science and philosophy and politics and even fund-raising and promotion—stand tall in the service of God and man and who amid conflicting tides of current thought courageously champion the core-truths of Biblical theism. A great alumni magazine that unfolds the drama of this intellectual and spiritual and moral engagement as it impinges upon contemporary civilization could become one of an evangelical college's best promotional voices.

Let's hoist a new standard of promotion and fund-raising. Let's be nothing more or less than God's trusted guardians of Christian doctrine and morality, certainly in Christian colleges, but equally in every other evangelical institution.

PART FIVE:

CONFRONTING
NEO–PAGANISM

FOURTEEN

THE CHRISTIAN WORLDVIEW IMPERATIVE

Every human being is born into some cultural context. None of us can choose, moreover, into which cultural setting he or she will emerge to life on earth. Inevitably a cultural given impinges on us. We learn a particular language in a particular historical age. If we move to another country, a different context of humanly shared beliefs, ideals, and institutions awaits us. Nobody lives in a cultural vacuum except an exile sealed off from society.

I

Many modern scholars jumble these realities into a theory of cultural relativism, and they seek to invert any claim for the once-for-all significance of Judeo-Christian revelation.

Some argue that since even Scripture comes to us in historically conditioned languages and in particular historical contexts it cannot convey absolute truth about God, redemption, or anything else. The argument is self-refuting. If it be true, then nobody—not even the critic—can tell us the truth about anything. Truth is in fact carried not by isolated words or linguistic fragments but by sentences; the historical particularity of words does not destroy the validity of propositional statements.

Still other critics—notably Professor George Lindbeck of Yale University—contend that all religions are cultural-linguistic phenomena, and that the only culture-transcendent religious knowledge available to us is mythical in nature. Religions, it is said, contain no revelatory truths but are diverse schemes of organizing human beliefs and behavior; Christianity is but one of a large class of cultural-linguistic models.

But Professor Lindbeck hardly demonstrates that Christian orthodoxy is mythical or false; he superimposes upon the data in advance a cultural-linguistic theory that requires a destructive conclusion. Moreover, if he actually gives us the transcendent truth about religion, his theory that we have only mythical data about transcendent reality is false. The theory is invalid in any event, even on Lindbeck's premises, since Lindbeck rules out objective truth about religious reality.

For all that, to insist that culture does not influence the world's religions would be foolhardy. One need only read Romans 1:23-25 for a devastating Biblical criticism of corrupt ancient Gentile religions. The main world religions of the present differ notably in what they affirm about spiritual truth and religious behavior and experience. The Great Divide between Biblical theism and other religions lies in the Judeo-Christian claim to once-for-all divine revelation and salvation by divine grace.

Yet Christians have no ground for contending that they are immune to the contaminating influence of the neo-pagan beliefs of today's secular culture. Just as the Hebrews were denounced by the inspired prophets in Old Testament times for compromising the divine law through concessions to pagan belief and practice, so in the New Testament the Apostle Paul criticizes the misbehavior of Corinthian Christians and urges the Christians at Colosse not to taper their worship and conduct to the prevalent speculative philosophies.

The Church in the modern world is confronted on many sides by naturalism or humanism and is under constant pressure to modify her Biblical commitments on monogamous marriage, abortion, divorce, and sexual behavior. Nor is that all. Her very mindset is often influenced by an academic milieu that is humanistic rather than theistic in approach, and her willset readily tapered to the behavioral stance of secular society.

The ancient Hebrews, living as they did in a theocratic society, had every reason to withdraw from Gentile neighbors. Christians, by contrast, are thrust into a pluralistic world as light, leaven, and salt. For New Testament Christians, neither the Essene Caves nor radical Anabaptist segregation from society can be a desirable option. The Christian mandate was not merely "be not conformed to this world" (Rom. 12:2), but also "sanctify the Lord God in your hearts, and be ready always to give an answer to every man that asketh you a reason for the hope that is within you . . ."(1 Pet.

3:15). Mankind was created in God's image and was assigned stewardship or dominion over the earth to preserve it for Yahweh's creational intention. The task of the people of God is, as far as possible in a sinful society, to reclaim the cosmos for God's created purpose.

In a fallen society, human culture is a sinful response to divine revelation. Were mankind, like the animals, unendowed with the *imago Dei,* there would be neither civilization nor culture. But the God of creation confronts mankind everywhere in His general revelation in nature and history and in the universally shared divine image. Mankind is Logos-lighted (John 1:9); sinful humanity clouds and obscures that light, but is unable to extinguish it (John 1:5). The world religions and secular philosophies respond to that light in the context of moral rebellion and without the guidance of special Scriptural revelation.

II

The Christian task in the world includes that of calling to account the cultural milieu in view of God's revealed Word, and that of exhibiting the New Society's regenerate community life reflecting the wisdom, righteousness, and joy of serving the one true God.

In two senses the Church therefore goes counterculture. First, she disputes not only the corrupt practices but also the alien beliefs about God and ultimate reality that inspire non-Biblical perspectives on life and the world. Second, she challenges the notion that a good society and just state can in fact be permanently sustained by unregenerate human nature. Christian culture presupposes both the Christian world-life view and the dynamic vitalities of spiritual regeneration.

That is not to say that Christianity can in fact achieve a flawless Christian culture in fallen history. To insist on a Millennium, in which Christ at His return in power and glory establishes His transcendent Kingdom on earth, is one thing. Quite another is the notion that Christians prior to the eschatological end-time can successfully achieve a truly Christian culture in a society that is universally infected by the consequences of original sin, and in which Christians themselves are limited by their own fallibility and foibles. For good reason Christianity rejects confidence in an immanent world-historical purpose in the form of inevitable evolutionary progress and shaped by human ingenuity as the bearer of universal salvation. It views historical activity rather as awaiting its future eschatological climax.

Yet Christianity does not wholly seal off "sacred history" from "world history." It challenges the latter in view of original sin and in view of a possibility of divine redemption. If Christians are not to be immersed in secular culture, neither are they, at the other pole, to be only hostile to culture. Christianity is, in fact, sometimes thought of only as a countercultural force, a premise encouraged by the tawdry manifestations that the secular world considers cultural. But Christianity is above culture, not anticulture nor pro-culture as such. Christianity is neither a superlative manifestation of secular history, nor is it so transcendent in principle that culture is a matter of indifference.

To strive for Christian culture is one thing; however, to affirm that Christians can achieve *a* pristine Christian culture in fallen history is quite another. We had best reconcile ourselves to the fact that in fallen history not even the regenerate Church will elaborate an unqualifiedly normative systematic theology, or Christian philosophy of law, or of literature and the arts. At best, Christians will achieve something less than the ideal, something always answerable to the Biblical revelation as the decisive criterion, even if the effort is devoutly made by the evangelical community or fellowship of the redeemed.

The difference here intended between Christian culture and *a* Christian culture is that the latter conception is comprehensive and all-embracing, such as that professedly achieved by medieval Catholicism. But the realities are that Christian cultural achievement is always something less than absolute. For that matter, instead of there being one universally ideal Christian culture, legitimacy may even be claimed for varieties of Christian culture, simply because the Church is transnational and transracial. In every cultural context the Christian community should seek to elaborate Christian culture vis-a-vis the antichristian or subchristian culture that engulfs it, and it should moreover seek to permeate secular society with the ideals and vitalities and realities of Christian culture. Christian culture-claims are more dynamic if they challenge and confront the contemporary alternatives.

A frequent complaint against evangelical Christianity is that it is really disinterested in cultural concerns. There can be little doubt that, during the fundamentalist-modernist clash in America, evangelicals burdened one-sidedly with evangelistic and missionary duties unfortunately withdrew from the public arena, a retrenchment that I protested in *The Uneasy Conscience of Modern Fundamentalism* (1947). The attraction of Roman Catholicism for some young evangelicals does not lie in its doctrine of papal infallibility and its Mariolatry, but in its literary engagement with secular society and its long cultural heritage. To be sure, the latter is often romanced; it was actually more of a nineteenth-century reality than it is a contemporary expression. The creative forces in Roman Catholicism today are seriously divided. But the need of evangelical cultural engagement remains in large part an unfulfilled task. Alexander Solzhenitsyn, C. S. Lewis, and Charles Colson, so often quoted approvingly by contemporary evangelicals, really did not have evangelical roots, but by God's grace have addressed legitimate cultural concerns that evangelicals largely have overlooked.

III

It makes a critical difference whether or not one thinks and acts christianly.

If one believes that God is the supreme Sovereign, one will not be deluded by myths about Hitler or Stalin or Mao or by emperors like the Roman caesars or the German Kaiser Wilhelm, who proclaimed "Deutschland über Alles!"

If one believes that God is creator of the planets and stars, one will pity sun-worshipers and horoscope addicts and all who think that human life is merely a cosmic accident.

If one believes that God created humanity in the divine image, one will not consider women inferior to men, or give credence to apartheid and myths about racial superiority.

If one believes that God instituted monogamous marriage—so that father, mother, and offspring conceived in wedlock form the ideal home—one will think differently about the single woman who wants a child outside of marriage, and about artificial insemination of a woman with the sperm of an unknown father.

If one believes that God fixes the boundaries of the nations, one will know that it is not military might alone that ultimately will decide the fortunes of the United States or Soviet Russia or Mainland China and Hong Kong.

If one believes that God is omniscient, one will not think one can hide the way one does one's business, or that what one does in the privacy of one's own home can be hidden.

If one believes that God made human beings to think His thoughts after Him, one will not stock one's soul with salacious literature or steep his spirit in pornographic publications.

If one believes that God intends the human body to be a temple of the Holy Spirit, one will not debilitate it with alcohol and cigarettes and drugs.

If one believes that God works out for good whatever touches the life of His children, one will not respond as pagans do to the loss of a job, to terminal illness, or to the unexpected death of a loved one.

If one believes that God commands us to love our neighbors as ourselves, one will not leave a neighbor in need or trouble to fend for himself or herself, but will treat the neighbor as extended family.

IV

For all that, the Christian must not stop with the recitation of a list of impressive moral particulars. Exposition of the Christian world-life view is a necessary priority for a comprehensive cultural thrust. It might seem to some readers that the importance of a Christian schematic perspective need only be mentioned in order to hurry along to the main task of cultural engagement. But that would be a serious mistake. Evangelicals—most of their prestigious institutions included—have made more of a promotional gimmick of an evangelical world-life view than a hard-won intellectual statement of its basic elements. Even less have they succeeded in expounding its implications for rival and conflicting contemporary alternatives.

One need not think long before identifying authors who profess to speak Biblically on different sides of Christian concerns and yet do not convincingly derive their emphases from Scripture. Some evangelicals contend that the Bible is irrelevant to cosmology. A recent evangelical volume on Christian world-life view says little about special divine revelation and much about theistic evolution. Another evangelical work on psychology scarcely mentions the soul. A well-known evangelical sociologist thinks that his discipline should be pursued solely on secular premises. Another thinks that Marx gives a more significant social analysis than do the Biblical prophets.

The serious task of world-life view elaboration is fundamental to significant cultural impact and application. It is astonishing that evangelical campuses engaged in the battle for the contemporary mind and will should so widely have neglected it in all but elementary ways.

One cause of this neglect has been the fact that anti-intellectual tendencies have influenced the evangelical community. Evangelistic success more than the victory of truth has become the goal of some campuses. A recent emphasis is that the *imago Dei* in mankind should not be identified as in evangelical theology traditionally with man's rational and moral capacities, but rather with his creative imagination. The emphasis on man's rational nature is held to be Greek rather than Hebrew. Personal truth in the form of myth, or of poetry and art, is championed as equivalent to or as superior to objective propositional or doctrinal revelation. Biblical truth, it is emphasized, is to be "done" rather than known in objective propositions. Hence the emphasis comes to serve a revolt against propositional revelation and to import political activism into the academic arena—often in behalf of leftist causes at that—as more important than traditional liberal arts concerns. Parents who are grateful that their offspring are publicly engaged rather than privately devoted to addictive drugs often buy this dubious emphasis unawares.

A comprehensive world-life view will embrace not only isolated consequences, but will bear on the whole of existence and life and supply the presuppositions upon which an orderly and consistent Christian involvement can be based. Just as the Enlightenment in its revolt against Biblical theism sought to explain law, religion, science, ethics, and all aspects of culture without reference to miraculous revelation and redemption, so Christian supernaturalism must bring into its purview every sphere of reality and activity. It will involve all the disciplines of a liberal arts education—the whole range of philosophical and moral thought, the sphere of education, literature and mass media, politics and economics, physical and biological sciences, psychology, leisure and the arts, and much else.

V

Before Christians can effectively shoulder their cultural task in the world at large, it is imperative for the Church as the New Society of the redeemed—the cadre of the redemptively committed—to find for herself the community worldstyle and lifestyle that marks believers off from the world. It counts little when a vanguard confronts secular society with demonstrations and calls for options that in fact are not widely entrenched in the community of faith.

Those who view the Church as merely a parenthesis in the outworking of the world-historical succession of empires will understandably balk at the idea of Christian culture as an external social phenomenon and favor the Church's remoteness from present-day historical reality.

Yet one reason secular society so easily modifies the thought and practice of the Church is that all too little comprehensive dialogue is underway, all too little effort that addresses such concerns as what constitutes good literature or good art, how one's vocational gifts can contribute to Christian culture, what moral responsibility has the inventive scientist for the deployment of his discoveries to barbarian ends, what makes recreation truly recreative, and so on.

The Bible does not—for example—say much about aesthetics (as we understand the term) and for good reason. But evangelicals have long said even less, and in the present cultural context they pay heavily for this neglect. In recent decades, however, there has been a developing evangelical interest in art and aesthetics, not without risks.

Many commentators remark that the Old Testament is unconcerned with beauty as an aesthetic quality and has a low estimate of art. Beauty is viewed in the context of the Creator's divinely ordered universe: the beautiful is what appropriately fulfills God's purpose, not merely individual experience of something visibly pleasing or evocative of admiration. As Calvin indicates, the created universe is a theatre for God's glory. The beauty of birds and flowers and trees and hills is seen in the context of their Maker, apart from whom everything withers and vanishes. It is mankind as the image of God and God's revelation in nature that constitutes creational beauty, which sinful rebellion mars and obscures. Graven images or replicas of God spatialize and temporalize the Deity by melding the Creator and the created. The visual experiences—such as cloud and fire—focus attention on the transcendent Lord; only in the Incarnation is God seen "in the flesh" and here not in symbol merely but in historical actuality.

The modern focusing of beauty only in terms of visual gratification reflects the fragmented experience of a generation adrift from comprehensive meaning. There is nothing ethically neutral about the Old Testament conception of beauty. The Bible associates beauty with worship and divine purpose and righteousness. This is a far remove from the modern emphasis on "art for art's sake" and the complete subjectification of meaning in art and its isolation from the attestation of God's glory.

VI

What can be done to facilitate the correlation of the Christian world-life perspective with all the realms of reality and life?

Intellectually the college faculties represented in the Christian College Coalition in counsel with evangelical faculty personnel on major secular campuses might well coordinate cognitive resources in every discipline of learning in periodic conferences aimed at advancing a world-life overview that pointedly addresses the contemporary scene.

A national Christian art competition might be sponsored in connection with the Christian Booksellers Convention, or a national Christian literature competition for evangelical fiction, especially historical novels that reflect modern social dilemmas and the tension and conflict between divergent value-systems. The Evangelical Press Association, in connection with its annual convention, might reward the best evangelical literary contribution to appear in the secular media.

There is not a sphere of learning and life that should fall outside the Christian vision. To be sure, secular spirits will criticize the evangelical "invasion" of any arena in which humanists have firmly entrenched themselves. They will see every countermove as a threat to tolerance and as an attempt to restore theocracy. But the best safeguard of cultural tolerance and the best barrier to state absolutism is the New Testament itself. Surely the atheistic totalitarian powers are not paragons of tolerance. One need not be intolerant of all behavioral pluralism in secular society just because one protests the rampant moral deviation that increasingly characterizes Western society. But the current condition of the secular milieu calls insistently for an exhibition of evangelical culture that confronts contemporary human alienation from God and man with a vital alternative. Never has the need for a culture enlivened by the moral law of God been more urgent than in our generation when social tumult obscures the very patterns of normalcy, and in fact increasingly champions the normless. In a culture dominated by a neo-pagan mind and will, deviation tends to become the norm, and normalcy in turn is perversely declared deviant. That cultural condition is the midnight hour for an evangelical alternative that seeks to count for something significant before the collapse and ruination of the contemporary social scene.

FIFTEEN

THE CHRISTIAN SCHOLAR'S TASK IN A STRICKEN WORLD

The West has lost its epistemic and moral compass. It has done so, moreover, at the very time when the world more than ever is aware of its intellectual and ethical diversity, and when a possibility of nuclear destruction overhangs the cultural crisis. Our awesome imperative as scholars is to address the civilizational turmoil of Euro-American culture.

Western society is now engulfed by neo-pagan naturalists who consider impersonal cosmic processes and events their homeland. These intellectual frontiersmen, as they would like to be known, disdain theological themes as a diversionary concession to abstract word games. Many in our generation are unsure of the sense and worth of human life. They hold in suspense, moreover, distinctive values of Western civilization, such as the ultimacy of God the Creator, the equal dignity of human beings, a divine purpose in nature and history, the supreme manifestation of righteousness and love in Jesus of Nazareth, and a final triumph of the good and decisive judgment of evil. These fundamentals and their implications are now vigorously assailed by the radical secularism that formatively influences education, the mass media, and politics.

We are well aware that Biblical theism supplied the cognitive supports of Western culture. It adduced a linear view of history; it affirmed the sacredness of human life; it focused man's responsible role as steward of the cosmos; it nurtured the development of modern science; it engendered the compassionate humanitarian movements that differentiated Western society; it shaped the vision of a climactic end-time triumph of the good and of mankind's decisive deliverance from injustice; it offered the practical impetus and a means as well of transforming human existence into a New Society that exudes moral and spiritual power.

This formative influence of Judeo-Christian motifs upon the outlook of the Western world is conceded by theistic and non-theistic scholars alike. Political theologian Johannes B. Metz affirms that "the Jewish and Christian Biblical message . . . first recognized the world as history."[1] Marxist philosopher Ernst Bloch grants that "all the utopian aspirations of the great movements of human liberation derive from Exodus and the messianic parts of the Bible."[2] The ultimate basis for belief in individual equality, observes John H. Hallowell, is the emphasis of the Biblical creation account on the dignity of all human beings as bearers of the image of God.[3] Alfred North Whitehead acknowledged that the Biblical view of nature's creation and preservation by a sovereign rational God contributed essentially to the emergence of modern science. The historian F. A. Foakes-Jackson affirmed that the humanitarian movements of the West all took their rise from the theology of the Cross. One could readily expand this avowal of our deep cultural indebtedness to Christianity.

The Christian view of God and the world, although not disproved, has nonetheless lost its grip on the mind of modernity, and many intellectually formative centers in the erstwhile Christian West now strip it of force. With the emergence of modern philosophy, speculative theists built a case for theism by appealing not to divine rational revelation and Biblical disclosure but rather to creative philosophical reasoning. Scientific empiricism, with its growing regard for sensory observation as the only authentic way of knowing, rendered suspect claims for the reality of the supernatural. Modern phenomenological theory stressed the knower's subjective contribution to experience; logical positivism confined truth and meaning to empirically verifiable claims; secular humanism openly proclaimed the modern victory of ancient naturalism. In the beleaguered culture of the West atheistic forces today hold a major initiative in universities, in the mass media, and in politics. Atheistic Communists rule over most of the earth's landmass; many countries long considered Christian remain under Soviet domination; most European nations claiming Free World status show meager interest in Christianity. In the United States, still the bulwark of global evangelism and missions, the neo-pagan left increasingly prods humanists to embrace an uncompromising naturalism.

Say what one will about its defection from historic Christian theism, the West's fall away from Biblical theology proved more costly than its promoters at first recognized. The naturalistic demotion of a supernatural deity to fable and fantasy had, of course, left a vacuum where medieval philosophers had long spoken confidently of eternal being, objective truth and good, creation, purpose in nature and history, sin and redemption, divine incarnation, spiritual regeneration, and universal moral judgment. But that was not all. However gradual, the intellectual transformation of traditional conceptions of cosmic reality and human history was far-reaching, and it produced new theories of man, of religion, law and ethics, and of much else.

The sacrifice of a personal and purposive Creator and Sustainer of the universe led to new cosmologies that left unsure man's substance and status in the cosmos. The deletion of a divine activity and goal exposed history and nature to unbridled speculation, whether about their creative new possibilities or about their inherent futility. As James H. Moorhead remarks, "Without God to relativize nature, the latter became a closed system of causal order in which human freedom and efficacy were problematic. Likewise, the absence of a God who endowed nature or history with purpose forced people to play gods themselves; and that Promethean quest forms the substance of the dismal stories of nationalism, Marxism, existentialism, and other variants of secular humanism. The result has been a 'blight of meaninglessness' plaguing Western culture."[4]

It has long been recognized that early modern speculative theists and the triumphant naturalists who succeeded them both unwittingly retained from Biblical theism some highly important emphases. To be sure, conjectural theism abandoned Scriptural revelation, discussed God's existence without reference to christology and apart from an articulate doctrine of man's sin, fall, and redemption. The cultural theists in the main shared with ancient classic idealism a speculative insistence on the reality of the supernatural, the supra-animality of man, and the objectivity of truth and good. Yet, in contrast with ancient supernaturalists, and under the influence of Christianity, even conjectural theists broke with the theory that matter is evil, and viewed the universe as somehow a divine creation, restated variously in terms of divine emanation, continuous creation, or evolutionary development. They clung also to the future Kingdom of God, although they increasingly grounded this expectation in notions of man's essential goodness and history's inevitable progress toward utopia. Instead of a universe pliable in the hands of its Creator free to act routinely or to work miracles, they spoke of God mainly as a phantom whose presence guaranteed a felicitous end-time.

Detached as it was from the self-disclosing God and from the power of an inscripturated revelation, conjectural theism—for all its retention of other fragments of Judeo-Christian teaching—could not hold the line against naturalism. Whatever their intentions, the theories forged by Kant and Hegel channeled into naturalism. For all his effort to rescue the universal validity of human knowledge, Kant deprived mankind of God's implanted image and allowed theism only postulational significance, whereas by making everything God, Hegel made God nothing. Slowly but surely speculative philosophy in the West collapsed into the theory that nature alone is real, that man is essentially only a complex animal, and that distinctions of truth and the good are temporary and changing.

For all that, the form in which modern exponents first championed naturalism was notably less radical than ancient Greco-Roman materialism. Post-Christian naturalism, no less than post-Christian theism, inadvertently borrowed from the Judeo-Christian heritage aspects of the Biblical worldview that are logically extraneous to atheistic empiricism. While early modern naturalism indeed affirmed nature to be ultimately real, it was prone to identify nature in terms of Reason—that is, of a mathematically structured system accessible to human observation and verification. It therefore assumed that man is somehow the apex of nature, and indeed permanently so, and also that distinctions of truth and morality, while subject to change, could through empirical confirmation nonetheless gain a relatively durable significance.

The notable point then is that the Christian revelational world-life view had so deeply penetrated the mind and conscience of Western man that both modern speculative theism and early modern naturalism, despite their deliberate rejection of Judeo-Christian fundamentals, remained more deeply dependent on unique Biblical emphases than either movement suspected. That same haunting indebtedness is true also of contemporary secular humanism; into its naturalistic control-beliefs it infuses a social agenda of durable imperatives including concern for the poor and weak and for universal justice. But if reality reduces ultimately to impersonal, purposeless processes and events, if man is the accidental by-product of a cosmic explosion, and if man creatively defines and redefines the content of truth and the good, then no consistent place remains for unrevisably fixed ethical norms. Critics often note that while radically secular humanism has sacrificed the metaphysical realities that make sense of moral absolutes, it nonetheless affirms certain absolutes despite their incongruity with naturalistic presuppositions; this it does, moreover, because secular humanism has been unable to divest itself wholly of Judeo-Christian influence. The Biblical view of the world, as Thomas Dean observes, has "proved decisive in the subsequent shaping of the Western outlook, both the world of Christendom and the world of modern secular man."[5]

Today radically secular humanism is increasingly placed on the defensive by evangelical criticism on the right and by neopagan secularism on the left. Speaking already over twenty years ago, Herman Dooyeweerd observed of the European scene that "the Humanistic faith in *mankind,* and in the power of human reason to rule the world and to elevate man to a higher level of freedom and morality, has no longer any appeal to the mind of the present day mass man. . . . This modern man . . . considers himself cast into a world that is meaningless, and that offers no hope for a better future."[6] A widening tradition of hard-core naturalism shuns the humanist commitment to universal human welfare and finds no basis for confidently viewing man or society as specially important. Those who espouse a purely scientific view of persons, and are prone to explain mind and consciousness in neurophysiological terms, have little basis for insisting on the dignity of humanity.

Revelatory theists have long stressed that secular humanism's social agenda is merely a cut-flower phenomenon doomed to wither for lack of metaphysical roots, and that it cannot logically withstand the rapid deterioration of cultural norms. If impersonal processes comprise reality, naturalism has no consistent basis for identifying man as the evolutionary capstone, let alone for adducing universal and permanent human rights, or for championing the weak and impoverished rather than affirming the survival of the fittest. To take evolution seriously, some stress, as did Bertrand

Russell, is to concede that eventually the human species will be as insignificant in the context of some yet future emergent as the primal protozoa or single-cell animal is today considered inconsequential; in an atheistic evolutionary context the fixed nature of man and the permanence of present-day human rights seem indefensible. The evolutionary prospect of a superman or superspecies renders problematic the universality of human rights; in the framework of German National Socialism, Adolf Hitler considered Aryans as inheritors of the future and Jews as inferior species unworthy of preservation.

Marxist materialistic metaphysics likewise presumes to account for all physics, history, ethics, politics, and economics. It links with a supposedly altruistic social program its view that the totalitarian state originates all human duties and rights. Not without reason is communism sometimes declared to be a "Christian heresy." Biblical futurism enters into its distortive dogma that history will eventually crest in a proletarian Communist utopia. But failure of the Russian Revolution to attain its promised utopia has necessitated a critical revision of the Communist dogma that the universe is self-enclosed and governed by inviolable mechanical necessity.

Radical secularism rejects the view of Greek philosophers and of Spinoza and Hegel that the world-process is a self-sufficient totality in which all entities arise through a reorganization of what already exists. Instead, it gratuitously borrows from the Bible the emphasis that the universe is open to transformation, and is not self-enclosed or governed by mechanical determinism. In unwitting dependence on Biblical truth, it holds to the possibility of the new creation of an open future. To be sure, secularism discards as myth the Biblical doctrine that the universe owes its existence to an independent, transcendent, personal Creator. It does not relate cosmic contingency to ontological dependence on a supernatural Creator; rather, it characterizes the universe itself as ungrounded continuous creativity, as free activity capable of being channeled toward a revolutionary humanization of mankind.

Against cosmic and historical determinism, Christian-Marxist dialogue has posed anew the question of human self-transcendence. Many neo-Marxists now affirm the openness of nature and history to the future, and emphasize that human decision and praxis are necessary to the triumph of the Communist dialectic.

These neo-Marxists pursue a restatement of the doctrines of nature, man, and history in a dialogue that attests that, even while post-Christian speculation slides ever more deeply into neo-pagan atheism, it nonetheless during this descent clings doggedly to ever-fading remnants of the Biblical view.

Across a half-generation scholarly exchanges have occurred between secular spokesmen who profess to speak on the one hand for a revised Christian view, and on the other for a critically-restated Marxist view. All these disputants consider themselves secular radicals; one side claims to speak christianly, although that description may be debatable. Both sides repudiate a supernatural ontology and insist on a one-layer finite reality.

Marxism, as we know, considers the Christian doctrine of God to be merely an ideological reflection of man's alienation from his fellowman. In the Christian priority for God Marxism sees a preoccupation with individual redemption, a devaluation of the world, and a passivity concerning the *status quo*. Atheism is basic to Marxist humanism. It therefore scorns the mediating effort of socially-minded theologians to so revise the Biblical view that a supernatural Deity supports materialistic humanism and this-worldly priorities.

No less than secular neo-Marxists, the more radical "Christian" secularists also abandon any supernatural reality, and along with this forego the divine creation of the finite cosmos, and the center of history in Jesus of Nazareth. In short, they surrender any conceptual equivalent of the supernatural God of the Bible. In contrast to Paul Tillich's Ground of all being, Charles Hartshorne's bi-polar divinity, and Gustavo Gutierrez's politicizing of revelatory motifs into a revolutionary eschatology, the "Christian" secularists join Marxists in renouncing every effort to modernize a supernatural reality. Instead, they exchange a theistic ontology outright for a finite world as the ultimate horizon of human life and destiny.

In this so-called "Christian"-Marxist debate neo-Marxist philosophers diverge, as we have said, from the orthodox Communist dogma of materialistic and collectivistic determinism which excludes the new in nature and history. To be sure, neo-Marxism coordinates social revolution with the naturalistic insistence on process, temporality, and change; but it does so in an existential context around which its discussion of theism, atheism, and humanism then revolves. It reintroduces a measure of transcendence, and undergirds revolutionary and utopian expectation by linking human freedom with historical openness to an earthly future.

The radically "Christian" secularist similarly stresses human autonomy and responsibility for restructuring society amid pervasive anxiety and alienation. He rejects a deterministic reduction of humanity to merely physical or biological data, or even to only psychological and sociological data, and reaches beyond human finitude and existential experience to promote an anthropology that involves a realm of transcendence.

While in Paris and other Continental centers Christian secularists so-called and disenchanted Marxists dialogued over transcendence, radically secular humanists progressively penetrated public education, the media, and government in the Anglo-Saxon West. Secular humanism distanced itself from thoroughgoing naturalism by championing social justice and compassion, and by accommodating all religions and all the gods, supernatural or not—although it stripped the entire panoply of objective significance. To religion it assigned a functional role, one that brought subjective integration to the alienated self, and thus supplied beleaguered human experience with a unifying perspective. According to secular humanism, religion tells the "truth" insofar as it integrates the discordant outlook of the embattled ego, but it *lies* if it professes to depict the objective nature of reality.

Modern philosophy progressively whittled down the essence of human personhood. The Biblical rational-moral self made in God's image gave way to Descartes' doubting ego, and then to Hume's stream of consciousness, until nothing remained but a terminally withered psyche. Conjectural philosophy snared the spiritually arid self in impersonal processes that offered little prospect but mechanical determinism.

Neo-Marxists and radically "Christian" secularists challenged the ancient doctrine of deterministic recurrence. The neo-Marxist alternative to mechanical determinism combines human creativity with an obscure overriding of cosmic necessity. But the debate over man's cosmic and historical transcendence vis-a-vis an all-encompassing determinism reflects a much deeper disorder. The disavowal of theism invited the decline of both idealism and humanism to unqualified naturalism. Neither the projection of an altruistic society nor the projection of a revolutionary utopia can long outrun a purposeless cosmos and history.

No doubt mankind has a melancholic sense of meaningless-ness, a pervasive experience of alienation, a capacity for self-criticism, a haunting awareness of death. No doubt human aspirations and needs reach beyond the socioeconomic. But to explain these elements in terms of an ontology of finitude tapers the discussion of man's transcendence to his being-in-this-world without acknowledging his link to the supernatural. If it does not lead to God, the search for an obscure transcendence beyond the self leads only to despair; self-transcendence—or the self beyond itself—is a self in serious psychiatric trouble.

Augustine's confession of a larger spiritual reality, "Thou hast made us for Thyself, O God, and our hearts are ever restless until they find their rest in Thee," represents the only supreme wisdom about man's ego. Any lesser position forfeits the only referent that can relativize either cosmic recurrence or human decision. For man and society the loss of Biblical theism means the loss also of genuine liberation and humanism. The view of so-called radical "Christians" and revisionary Marxists who contend that Christian theism is theoretically untenable and Marxists who contend that Judeo-Christian ontology deforms the essential nature of human life can only mislead us; for their view of human existence is not only shallow and incomplete, but also false. Promoting naturalistic boundaries of existence, the "Christian" and Marxist secularists deny that any conceptual-logical framework extends beyond finite realities; their obscure notions of transcendence lack any nonfinite mode of reality. The self-styled radical "Christian" abandons those very theistic realities that best illumine the borders of the finite at the very edges where naturalism becomes mystical and ambiguous.

The frayed remnant of anthropological transcendence that secularists affirm is but the death rattle of an expiring theism whose strangulation neo-paganism eagerly anticipates. Since its rupture with Biblical revelation, secular Western philosophy has progressively stripped away Christianity's arms and legs and head and heart—namely, its transcendent Creator, its purposive universe, its goal in history, and its unique incarnation of the Logos in Jesus Christ. Not even plastic surgery could restore ontic significance to Karl Barth's transcendent revelation once he deemed public reason irrelevant to revelatory truth. Agreeing with Barth that God remains real only in personal decision, Bultmann capitulated outright to the secular worldview. Unimpressed by the theological subtleties of European theologians and metaphysicians, hard-core naturalism unqualifiedly repudiated theistic ontology and insistently made scientism its creed.

Western culture today overwhelms all other cultures; its interpreters promote its reductionist worldview around the globe. In consequence, as Lesslie Newbigin says, the scientific worldview has become "the operative plausibility structure of our modern world."[7] Demanding that all disciplines submit their truth-claims to its judgment, the scientific worldview relativizes all presuppositions but its own. Its restrictive methodology tolerates neither divine revelation nor miracle, neither design in nature nor purpose in history; it thus guarantees that Biblical theism will be rejected as a publicly-significant option. At the same time scientism is hospitable to Asian religions that reject a Creator/creation distinction and that encourage the theory that all religions are essentially one.

But there is another, and equally important, side to this reductionist assault. It is that Western culture itself, where this reductionist view first took root, is becoming more impervious to Christian influences than are African and Asian cultures. Posttheistic atheism stands guard against any tatters of transcendence that derive genetically and logically from the Judeo-Christian heritage. Stripped of futurist illusions, the reinvigorated pagan spirit collapses even the anthropological transcendence of Christian-Marxist dialogue into historical cycles and cosmic determinism. It regards the Biblical inheritance in its totality as antiquated. Christianity is considered destructive of self-fulfillment; its effort to alter human dispositions is deplored as an inexcusable tampering with natural instincts; its commendation of the survival-rights of the weak is declared misleading; sin is considered an illusion whose admission leads to neurosis; the call to regeneration is regarded as repressive of man's cultural identity.

Over against Christianity, atheistic materialism deliberately sets forth its genius as definitive of the truly civilized mind and energetically thrusts raw naturalism into the cultural mainstream. Rooted in the rebellious spirit of fallen man, nurtured in the past by Greco-Roman materialistic cosmology, reinforced by post-Renaissance humanism, neo-naturalism considers the Protestant Reformation an intellectual catastrophe. Claiming to be Europe's authentic heritage, it disparages classic idealism, medieval trinitarianism, and modern philosophical theism as suppressants of the genius of naturalism.

Ever since Nietzsche, the pagan motif has captivated ardent literary luminaries, among them Hermann Hesse, Julian Huxley, Aldous Huxley, D. H. Lawrence. In this century, the spirit of paganism first scaled the walls of civilization to gain a foothold here and there; today it is deeply entrenched in the cultural enterprise. Ours is, as Newbigin says, no longer "a secular society. It is a pagan society, and its paganism, having been born out of the rejection of Christianity, is far more resistant to the gospel than the pre-Christian paganism with which cross-cultural missions have been familiar."[8]

Martin Heidegger critiques all Western onto-theology, Biblical theism no less than the speculative isms, whose destiny in common is from the outset, he says, the cultural death of God conceived as an object. From their beginnings, he protests, Greek metaphysics and Christian theology misguidedly postulated a supreme existence as the basis of everything else, a foundation deeper than the actually given existence of reality. Heidegger invites theology to say what it can on the basis only of revelation as an irreducible event. Although Heidegger does not intend his philosophy to be deployed theologically, it nonetheless carries preconceptions important for theism. Heidegger's questioning of being and his search for a nonobjectified reality would seem to reduce Deity, as Claude Geffré implies, to "the other party without content in an encounter about which nothing can be said."[9]

In Heidegger's aftermath so-called deconstructionist philosophers, paced by Jacques Derrida, demand the dismantling of the entire Western tradition of philosophy and theology, with its emphasis on objectively existing Deity. Setting out anew from the pre-Socratic thinkers, they propose an anti-Logos course, under whose influence, notes Geffré, "the theologians themselves eagerly echo such phrases as 'the end of metaphysics,' 'the death of the god of metaphysics,' 'the end of theism,' and 'the beginning of a post-metaphysical age.' "[10]

Karl Barth's elevation of the actuality of God above the logical law of contradiction is welcomed as an unwitting contribution to the deconstructionist effort.[11] Religious ontology is declared lacking in cognitive basis, is derogated as mere human imagination, in the name of a revolution in consciousness that replaces the Judeo-

Christian theological heritage by what Lonnie D. Kleiver calls a polysymbolic fictive religiosity. Nietzsche, Heidegger, and Derrida are prime movers in this effort to deconstruct and then to radically reconstruct the very history of Western thought through a new attitude toward reality and a new methodology. The deconstructionists reject the dominance of culture both by mathematico-scientific thought (with its quantitative-atomic approach to reality) and by the "onto-theo-logical" tradition of Western philosophy and theology (with its personal divine object). Hegel's *Phenomenology of Spirit* accelerated interest in a dialogical activity and a new language system in which reality emerges in conversation. Nietzsche displaced supernatural Deity by the will to power, and detached the divine image in man from both reason and will. Derrida seeks to banish not only the "Greco-Christian God," but to strip away also any eternal and immutable Logos—any "logocentrism"—that permeates the universe. He seeks release from formal logic and from the desire for verification, and projects an evolving fluid logos and open spectrum of verbal signification. The one sure result is a nihilistic assault on the Judeo-Christian heritage; no longer does the word god refer to a singularly unique metaphysical being. Max A. Myers proposes to replace the term "theology" by the term "religious thinking."[12] For Myers, god is a cluster of linguistic names and images whose meaning waits to emerge within dialogic activity.[13] In Carl A. Raschke's words, "The deconstruction of god coincides with the end of theology. . . . Reconstruction is the dance of death upon the tomb of God."[14]

We would misread the self-styled deconstructionist movement if we totally disdain its repudiation of Western metaphysical theology. In view of the almost endless succession of new vogues in theology—the anthropological and post-positivist versions of theology in recent modern thought, the endless medieval theorizing about divine Being, the ready Greco-Roman objectification of conflicting deities—have not many of us believed also that for secular philosophy and theology wintertime was overdue? Raschke pointedly describes the vacuity of the modern outlook when he says that "the idols of the secular marketplace have a tinny ring" and that "the logos of our latter-day '---ologies,' including theology, has become naught but a ritualistic and compulsive defense against . . . 'the void.' "[15] The increasing entrapment of Deity in space-time processes, the ongoing religious reductionism bent on compressing Deity until God gives up the ghost, the attempt to derive a metaphysics from an analysis of finitude, are these not some of the many elements of a metaphysical menagerie by which Western intellectual thought has brought itself to an impasse? Surely a critical reexamination of metaphysical theorizing was needed, as well as a challenge also to the objectification of conflicting deities, and a reshaping of religious studies and their theological lifeline. The object of Christian theology is simply not Aristotle's Pure Act, Tillich's Ground of all being, or a score of modern alternatives.

Yet a much bolder concern motivates the deconstructionist movement. It considers all traditional metaphysics spurious, including Christian theology; it espouses not simply the deposition of twentieth-century intellectual history but also the liquidation of theology. Over against historic Christianity it sponsors a defection more radical than the Renaissance, a break with orthodoxy that requires the cancellation of Biblical theism, and the abandonment of the ontological reference of all theological language. We are told that all that has been said about the transcendent Creator-Redeemer God of the Bible needs to be dismantled as a conjectural misconception.

The element of truth in deconstructionism, that the metaphysical and theological tradition of the West calls for radical critique, is nullified by its intended dethronement of Biblical theism along with conjectural philosophy, and its deliberate espousal of an atheistic alternative. Neo-paganism counters the reality of the one God, counters confidence in divine creation, counters the gospel of divine redemption, counters the singular incarnation of the Logos in Jesus Christ.

The qualitative leap that deconstructionism champions is a life-or-death matter for theology, one that proposes a sweeping dehistoricizing of Biblical faith, one that confuses rather than clarifies a plausible system of reference for theological realities, one that substitutes a creative consciousness for intelligible divine disclosure. In the deconstructionist movement, atheism no longer entrenches itself as but one dissenting option among others, but rather as the epistemic center of human experience, the primal referent through which absolute emptiness replaces absolute being. Its public prospectus and agenda are ranged both against scientific rationalism with its technocratic illusion of utopia and against the Judeo-Christian heritage.

Neo-paganism rails against mind grounded in the Logos of

137

God, against reason per se as truth and reality. The logos now becomes only a thought-form in the human mind, a product of evolution and experience, whose asserted centrality is viewed not only as a disservice to theology but also to man himself. For some decontructionists logos is simply "a gathering of meaning in a dialogic event." Raschke writes of the transformation of word as *logos* ("representation") into word as *rhema* ("flow").[16]

Seldom is it so openly stated that this promotion of self-sufficient nature as an all-engulfing process strips history of linear meaning and purpose, sunders human life from fixed goals, and rejects universally shared reason. Neo-naturalism rejects all the professedly altruistic cultural and political models that stem from the so-called Christian heresies of communism and socialism. Rejecting the linear view of history as a sham, the neo-pagan spirit sees in Marxism but a secular version of Biblical messianism; it reverts to cyclical history and disowns a climax in the historical process. In the dogmatically formulated views of Jacques Monod *(Chance and Necessity*, New York: Random, 1972) and Carl Sagan *(Cosmos*, New York: Ballantine, 1985) this mechanistic mood speaks for contemporary academe.

Hard-core naturalists herald the repudiation of God, of a purposive creation, and of eternally fixed moral imperatives as the dawning of millennial freedom. "Nature is replete with its own rhythms," says philosopher Reuben Abel; its "periodicities are neither necessary, unique or eternal." He assures us that it is "adolescent folly" to think that "romantic despair, or nihilism, or radical skepticism" ensue "if there are no purposes in nature other than the ones we introduce; if *Homo sapiens* is merely the end product pro tem. of random mutations in certain chemicals" or if human personality cannot be clearly differentiated from the body.[17] Yet Abel does not show why his optimism may not also be the by-product of chemical mutants.

This mindshift from theism to naturalism does not mean that in the shaping centers of contemporary society Biblical theology is now a shattered encrustation. For many it remains the only form in which supernatural metaphysics retains credibility as an intellectual option. The two main lessons of twentieth-century theology are, first, that the concept of a personal God is viable only where God makes Himself known in self-revelation, and second, that only where the divine will is Scripturally encapsulated does divine revelation fully escape mystical generality and ambiguity.

This is not to deny universal revelation; the Bible itself insists that every human being has some knowledge of God and His claim on conscience. But, more clearly than ever, the cognitive conflict today reduces to Biblical theism or bald naturalism as the real alternatives; the intermediary options continue to collapse into ever-fading compromises. Say what one will about Christianity's loose grip on the secular mainstream, it retains herculean educational and ecclesiastical resources—television, radio, literature, professionally trained missionaries and clergy, and vocationally prominent lay leaders in all arenas of work. In the most powerful nation on our planet fifty million persons claim to be "born-again" Christians, and many have emerged from cultural isolation to remount a public and social witness.

But these advances largely bypass a challenge to the intellectual crisis. The electronic church in America, mass evangelistic crusades, and much pulpit oratory are concerned to challenge the will of contemporary man more than to confront the mind of modernity. Even evangelical colleges respond tardily to the need for competent exposition of the Christian world-life view, and some are becoming so concessive that critics consider them counterproductive in advancing Christian core-beliefs (cf. James D. Hunter, *Evangelicalism. The Coming Generation*, Chicago: University of Chicago Press, 1987). No great evangelical metropolitan university has emerged to engage secular academe in a cognitive exchange that bristles with intellectual drama.

Yet even within mainstream philosophical circles one discovers a new regard for theistic belief. The Society of Christian Philosophers has enlisted a surprising number of members and its *Faith and Philosophy* journal has won an impressive circulation among professional philosophers. Competent evangelicals hold key philosophy posts on numerous mainline campuses; one of them, Alvin Plantinga, has been invited to give the prestigious Gifford Lectures. Evangelical seminaries are burgeoning with students, evangelical churches are growing, hundreds of their young scholars have earned doctorates from leading universities in Biblically-related fields, evangelical divinity professors are returning to mainstream professional societies, and more and more are contributing quality books in theological studies.

But lest one fall into grand visions of evangelical awakening, it is well to catch one's breath in the secular city. The disconcerting fact, as Lesslie Newbigin writes, is that wherever Western culture now penetrates in the name of modernity, it dissolves faith in the supernatural and in the inherited religious beliefs, and not least of all in Christian affirmation.[18] Rejoice though we may over Christian resurgence in Mainland China despite the Cultural Revolution, or in Third-World spiritual growth in South Korea, Kenya and elsewhere, the hard fact remains that over half the Asian population lives under the control of atheistic communism and that no movement in the twentieth century has reflected greater numerical growth than has atheism. In Europe, both on the Continent and in Britain, church attendance is pathetically low. Multitudes remain unreached by evangelical literature even in India, the second most populous nation on our planet and the home of most English-language literates outside the Anglo-Saxon West.

Anti-theistic humanists hold a driving initiative even in Western culture. Newbigin is speaking not of the Communist world but of Western society when he states that "the most obvious fact that distinguishes our culture from all that have preceded it is that it is—in its public philosophy—atheist."[19]

Merely to gloat over culture-pervasive anxiety, its boredom and loss of meaning, would constitute an unworthy intellectual cop-out. If we aim to win only the psychologically depressed, the suicidal fringe of a neo-pagan society, then Christianity will erase the tough-minded intellectual rebels from its prospect list and grant them cognitive immunity from Christian truth-claims. We dare not imply that Christianity has nothing to say to the unyielding naturalistic ego, and that we can only stand by to await its sure descent into the abyss of meaninglessness.

The fact is, Christianity says something powerful not only at emotional frontiers, but also and especially at the cognitive zenith of contemporary naturalism. It is quite willing to hear out "the other side," to allow the atheist and relativist to plead their cause, and to note how they strain to accommodate and even to promote certain imperatives as inviolable. It is Sidney Hook and Paul Kurtz and others of their intellectual stance to whom the claim of supernatural revelation is to be confidently addressed. It is the humanist in his unsteady humanism, the naturalist in his unjustifiable naturalism, whom we must engage. We must do so, moreover, not simply as crusaders for evangelistic decision, appropriate as that may be in its time and place, but in confrontation of both mindset and willset. We must dispute the axioms of neo-pagan thought, unmask a disposition under no absolute constraint to oppose eternal truth and a fixed good, and exhibit the self-legislated limits within which scientific empiricism lays claim to all truth and reality. We remind a scientistic society that modern science owes its very life not to the Greek philosophers or to Chinese, Indian, and even Egyptian sages with their noteworthy achievements in mathematics. Although self-imposed methodological limits constrain scientists to screen out supernatural reality and purpose, neither the interpretation of nature nor scientific necessity requires suspending them on empirical tolerances. We offer the pagan mind a critique of its illogic, of its incoherence and instability. We offer also a superior alternative—namely, the revelation of the personal Creator of a purposeful universe, and the incarnate Christ manifest in Jesus of Nazareth who stands tallest in the annals of humanity. We affirm this not merely as a matter of heroic courage, but confident that we are on the side of reason, that theistic claims stand the test of publicly-shared criteria, and that the Lord battles with us and for us.

The Christian world and life view is staggeringly comprehensive; its grand exposition embraces the whole of existence and life. The emerging naturalism of the West surrendered it stage by stage, unaware that its own quest for human meaning and worth rested upon borrowed premises. Christian theism deserves better from its friends than from its foes. In contemporary society it is the evangelical community that often obscures the comprehensive and cohesive nature of the Biblical view. Our colleges must recover the unifying character and explanatory power of revelatory theism. A sociology course that allows the *is* to determine the *ought*, a psychology course that merely sprinkles a few Scripture verses atop a secular theory of the self, a science course that views the creation account as poetic myth soon amputates all the vital parts until the whole is ready for cremation.

In view of the mounting financial pressures that threaten the effective survival of many colleges and universities, the fulfillment by the evangelical colleges of their distinctive educational mission becomes a major concern. This is all the more the case as Christian colleges seek to emulate the secular universities as evidence of professional maturity. There are no doubt some aspects of secular learning that faith-affirming institutions may well aspire to duplicate, and other aspects they had best avoid. A highly respected evangelical dean, Dr. Walter Kaiser, asks whether the time may not have come for the formation of an Evangelical Council for Academic Accountability which would function in educational matters much as the Evangelical Council for Financial Accountability functions in respect to promotional and fund-raising practices. Such an agency would ideally be independent of the Christian College Coalition and Christian College Consortium. It might be coordinated with the Commission on Higher Education of the National Association of Evangelicals. It would require an annual audit of academic fulfillment or nonfulfillment of publicly announced institutional principles and objectives, and stipulate the availability to the constituency of relevant records.

There is no good reason why the elaboration of Christian world and life postulates should be left to a cadre of gifted evangelical scholars in secular universities. The publications by Christian scholars in the secular world should be looked upon as a welcome stimulus to the entire evangelical academic community, prodding cooperative and corporate confrontation of secular modernity and modern consciousness. We need to wrestle the emerging neo-pagan agenda as a doomsday decision.

The worst affliction of the modern age is not AIDS, epidemic as it may be; atheism is, for it makes spiritual death unavoidable in this life and the next. For all that, AIDS is a plague that has arisen in a particular pagan era; its almost universal menace is a concomitant of a certain view of human life and its priorities.

The mindset of modernity is but a transitory phenomenon. But it will exploit the illusion of permanence if we do not effectively exhibit its weaknesses and more importantly exhibit the superiority of the theistic view. Modernity is but an agonizing moment in the history of civilizations; only a view that has eternal validity can hope to be forever contemporary. The transitional mindset is not worthy of one's soul. It is scientism—not science, or orderly knowledge of the natural world—that disqualifies secular consciousness; it is rationalization—not philosophy, or love of wisdom—that discredits secular consciousness; it is modern mythology—not theology, or the truth of God—that distorts secular consciousness. As the deconstruction of Western metaphysics gains momentum, it should be clear again that the enduring foundations of theology, philosophy and science rest upon the Biblical heritage. The loss of that Biblical heritage means the loss of one's soul, the loss of a stable society, and the loss of an intelligible universe as well. The intellectual suppression of God in His revelation has precipitated the bankruptcy of a civilization that turned its back on heaven only to make its bed in hell.

SIXTEEN

THE JUDEO-CHRISTIAN HERITAGE AND HUMAN RIGHTS

The contemporary crisis of law has stirred new interest in the taproots of justice and lively debate as well over the very basis of human rights.

The typically modern theories ignore divine law as the fundamental law. Because they lack accrediting metaphysical-moral ties, secular notions of jurisprudence collapse routinely into revered human convention. The Swiss jurist Peter Saladin comments that "the philosophical bases traditionally underlying the idea of human rights—the philosophical systems of the Enlightenment, of liberalism, of utilitarianism—are now crumbling and no longer credible. We can no longer cling to the anthropological optimism on which those systems rest without sacrificing our intellectual and moral honesty."[1] The French social critic Jacques Ellul insists that law in modern society is foredoomed to impotence unless law's transcendent revelatory foundations are revived.[2]

The central issues concerning the nature of law and of human rights become clear if we contrast the Biblical outlook with representations by other ancient Near Eastern religions, and with the medieval emphasis on natural law encouraged by Greco-Roman philosophy. The natural law perspective, in turn, was unable to resist the Enlightenment's detachment of all legal phenomena from divine revelation. Since then, the problem that has haunted naturalistic theory is that of locating for law and rights a transcendent ground that a merely empirical approach does not accommodate.

I. Human Rights in the Ancient World

The comparison of Biblical and ancient non-Biblical codes has often been flawed by conjectural assumptions. *Religionsgeschichte* scholars held that Old Testament law merely differentiates in an inferior way the perspectives of earlier Near Eastern cultures. Today, however, even many critical scholars have abandoned the search for earlier sources thought to provide a surer key to Hebrew religion and history than does the Bible. Also flawed was the view that the Bible's inspired character renders its reflections of law and justice superior at all points to Mesopotamian legal traditions. The Bible does present a distinctive law system grounded in singular theological premises that escape polytheism, astrology and magic. But Hebrew practice may not wholly have escaped the Chaldean culture in which Abraham was reared or the Egyptian culture in which Hebrews endured slavery.

Legal scholars long considered law codes of the ancient Near East of only incidental interest and focused mainly on their secondary and tertiary differences. But the ancient Near Eastern religions offer three distinctive conceptions of law and human rights: Mesopotamian, Egyptian and Hebrew. The basic contrast lies in the irreducible monotheism of Biblical religion and its unique cosmological, ethical and legal consequences.

Mesopotamian polytheism nullifies the absoluteness of a divine will, and it also jeopardizes the free expression of any and every god. It affirms primordial cosmic evil beyond control of the gods. Since there was primordial evil, the universe is uncontrolled by fixed moral principles. The gods, moreover, are not the source of truth and right. The panoply of divinities is not itself bound by shared moral principles, for the gods sometimes act unpredictably. Even if one of the gods demands justice from mankind, what is in view is not conformity to the will of a transcendent righteous deity but rather humanity's harmony with the cosmos. Non-Biblical religion has no once-for-all revelation and excludes the concept of a "covenant." The king's mandate to rule comes from the gods as rulers of the cosmos, but the king is obliged by them to conform all earthly life to the just cosmic order.

The Mesopotamian king is not a deity but a divine representative stationed between the gods and mankind, and his power is limited by an earthly assembly or political structure. These limitations on power preclude autocratic government and imply that human beings somehow have inalienable rights. Mesopotamian kings, therefore, like the Hebrew kings, were not the ultimate source of law but its guardians and servants. Since law was an extension of the divine cosmic order, obedience was a religious duty. But in the Mesopotamian view, it was the king or ruler who translated general principles of cosmic order into moral and legal particularities.

In Hebrew religion, by contrast, the one sovereign God freely creates the universe, fashions mankind in His rational-moral image, stipulates human duties, and holds humans responsible for discerning and doing His will. The Israelites recognized law as a revelation of Yahweh's will and not as a distillation only of a cosmic order to which gods also were answerable. Yahweh transcends not only part of the universe but the whole and controls nature for His sovereign ends, in contrast with a theogony of embattled deities who are part of nature. God is the only Legislator. Earthly rulers and legislative bodies are alike accountable to Him from whom stems all obligation—religious, ethical and civil. Yahweh supervises all human action; disobedience to Him is sinful. God rewards and punishes men and nations consistently with His revealed principles of justice and morality. Hebrew religion presented the one God not only as sovereign divine creator and judge, who made all mankind in His image to know revealed truth and morality, but as also personally disclosing His transcendent law in verbal specifics. In short, Hebrew religion spoke both of God's law and of God's word. The divine giving of the law at Sinai to the Hebrews as a covenant people is, as Martin Noth observes, a singular event that cannot be distilled from general religious history.[3] Here the transcendentally-given law is normative.

In contrast to a fixed cosmic order to which the Mesopotamian ruler was answerable in concert with the decision-making powers of a popular assembly, and in contrast to the Hebrew emphasis on the one sovereign Creator who is the source and articulator of law, the Egyptian legal system honored the Pharaoh as the sole source and living font of law. Absolute obedience was due the Pharaoh who ruled unlimited, not merely as a representative of the gods, or by divine right of kingship, but as inherently divine and personally endowed with justice. The Hebrews did not view their king as deity but as a representative of God bound by the law and possessing limited powers.

Hebrew Scripture constituted a trusted legal codex stating Yahweh's law in detail, whereas in Egypt, where each reigning pharaoh articulated it, law was not codified in a formal way; Egyptian language is said to have no term for generalized legal principles. But Jewish law has survived for more than three thousand years in various cultural and religious contexts as the oldest continually applied legal system in human history. That Yahweh's moral law is perpetually binding was reiterated by Jesus. The covenant-grounded Decalogue, summarizing the whole law, is phrased in direct commands ("You shall . . . You shall not . . ."), in contrast to the impersonal Mesopotamian law codes ("If . . . then . . ."). The Hebrews recognized no divine law independent of Scriptural law until, as Josephus says *(Antiquities,* 13.10, 6) the Pharisees promulgated oral traditions for which they proclaimed divine origin and authority.

A further distinctive of Biblical law must now be mentioned. Though it may at first seem astonishing to the contemporary mind, Jewish law, as Haim Cohn remarks, embraces no concept of human rights in the modern sense.[4] The Bible stresses "not rights but duties—and these were essentially duties to God," Louis Henkin reminds us, "although fellowman was the beneficiary of many of them."[5] The Bible does not teach that human beings simply on the basis of existence have inherent or *a priori* rights, or that they have absolute rights accruing from sociological or political considerations. The Bible has a doctrine of divinely imposed duties; what moderns call human rights are the contingent flipside of those duties. The Apostle Paul appeals to Caesar (Acts 25:11) not simply because Roman jurisprudence pledged a fair trial, but because Almighty God established civil government for the preservation of justice in fallen society (Rom. 13). While this renders problematical a doctrine of rights based merely on legal formality or social utility, it reinforces human dignity and the absoluteness of behavioral imperatives. To Christians in Rome Paul writes: "Owe no man anything but love," and then proceeds to give public content to love through the social commandments of the Decalogue (Rom. 13:8ff.). Yahweh formulates human duties as an obligation to God, not as conferring tangible rights or benefits upon humanity *per se.* Ultimately all duties reduce to two: love of

God with one's whole being, and under God love of others as ourselves. The Biblical theory divorces human rights discussion from metaphysical or sociological speculation and preserves it in the context of divine creation, divine disclosure, and present and future divine judgment.

A noteworthy exception to the Biblical concentration on duty rather than rights is the express stipulation of an accidental slayer's right to refuge from the blood avenger (Num. 35:11, 15; Deut. 4:42), although even here the right rests not on intrinsic human dignity but on the value God transcendentally assigns to human life.

To be sure, many Biblical duties—if not all—imply a corresponding enforceable right. The divine prohibition of theft or of removal of a landmark implies an unstated right to property and possession.

Yet the contrast between the Biblical and the modern approaches to human rights could not be more pointed. The Universal Declaration of Human Rights (1948) presents a panorama of human rights, while it says very little about human duties and nothing at all about duties to God. Only Article 29, which limits the exercise of rights by reciprocal rights and a regard for morality, public order and general welfare, refers to human duty, and even here the context is anthropological. Although the stipulated rights are considered the generally acknowledged norms of modern civilization, none is legally enforceable since the Declaration wholly ignores the subject of the ultimate source and sanction of rights and does not even obligate states to enact the stipulated rights. The Bible, by contrast, has no notion of publicly unobligated individuals who are beneficiaries of rights-claims, or of ultimate rights formulated and conferred by earthly institutions, let alone of civil government existing only as a humanly devised option. "Do unto others," said Jesus, "as you would that they do unto you" (Matt. 7:12).

The ancient Hebrew theocracy co-mingled civil and religious law; crime was punished both as a legal infraction and as sin. The theocracy incorporated not only the Decalogue with its universal social imperatives, but additionally imposed Yahweh's expectations from the Jews as His covenant-people. When the theocracy in time collapsed through Hebrew defection and exile, the way was prepared for a New Testament alternative: the people of Yahweh would be scattered worldwide to witness to God and His Christ in pluralistic societies. Crime would not lose its character as sin, but now civil government, as the divine instrumentality for the promotion and preservation of justice, would punish crimes against society; whereas the Church, as a transnational society evangelizing the earth and promoting spiritual redemption, would cope with sins against God.

Neither the inception nor the demise of the Hebrew theocracy nullified an original divine creational morality that universally survived original sin and the fall of humanity. This creational ethic included the institution of monogamous marriage, of work as a legitimate human activity, and of structures of authority. It presumably commanded in principle whatever the Decalogue enforces. Although the Biblical revelation resolutely protests against the religious orientation of Mesopotamia, the Old Testament introduces numerous legal practices as already existing. Primogeniture and inheritance were common in the Mesopotamian world, although divorce, polygamy and slavery also became widespread. Whether or not the Hebrews incorporated into the Biblical *corpus* fragments of Mesopotamian jurisprudence is not always clear; if so, what they borrowed may well have derived from creational morality or may have been accredited or refined by the light of special revelation. The Pentateuch's first and only reference to divorce, notably, requires the husband to give his divorced mate a bill of divorcement (Deut. 21:17). The Bible teaches that all human beings, irrespective of nationality or race or religion, have some intellectual and moral light and that conscience hails them anticipatively before God's judgment-throne. It condemns nonperformance of what humans know to be right as insistently as it deplores inexcusable ignorance of the right. The Old Testament condemns pagan Sodom for its neglect of the poor. Although Israel's neighbor-nations were without special revelation, Amos condemns them for treaty violations and brutality that transgressed creational morality. Traces of creational truth and ethics may therefore survive not only in certain similarities of the Babylonian Code of Hammurabi to the Old Testament. This is also seen in the Mesopotamian insistence that the source of law is transcendent to humanity and that all humanity is its servant, while yet the polytheistic disavowal of the one God forfeited the legal code as a direct divine word and command, substituting instead a human ruler's fallible conferral of verbal particularity on an impersonal cosmic order.

Nevertheless, the irreducibility of Old Testament law to non-Biblical law is evident in crucial features that concern murder, homicide and penal retribution. The Cain-and-Abel account depicts homicide as an offense to both God and society, one that violated Cain's duty to kin and neighbor (Gen. 4:8ff.). Whether or not Cain intended to slay Abel is unclear, but the emphasis on human accountability affirms a universal brotherhood of mankind (cf. Gen. 9:5). Genesis 9:1-6 virtually mandates capital punishment as the penalty for murder. Yet the divine image, which establishes human dignity, protects even the accused, who faces death not as an act of human revenge but because murder affronts the Creator who has fashioned humankind in His own image. The "covenant code" (Exod. 20—24) distinguishes accidental from deliberate killing, and provides sanctuary against mob violence or nonjudicial killing. Even the slayer of a slave is not exempt from the death penalty.

The law of retribution—"an eye for an eye" (Exod. 21:24ff.; Lev. 24:19ff.; Deut. 19:21) prevailed throughout the Near East, being found in the Code of Hammurabi (Sections 196—201). But the Babylonian and Biblical versions differ notably. We should recall that the Biblical creation account makes only one distinction within humankind, that between the sexes, and it does so to stress that both male and female are created equally in God's image. In the Bible the law of limits on retribution follows from the created equality of all human persons. In Scripture's only reciprocal application of the law, a ruler who had severed the thumbs and toes of captives was himself seized and similarly treated (Judg. 1:17). Scripture does not confer royal power of life and death upon rulers, but considers them answerable to God's justice.

The Biblical code prohibits bodily mutilation—such as cutting off arms, legs and noses—and limits flogging to forty strokes. Hammurabi's code is prone to regard the law of retribution as a stipulation of requisite penalty more than as a statement of limits. It requires greater retribution, moreover, for injury to a nobleman's son than to a commoner, and less than for a commoner if the injury is to a slave. Hammurabi's code prescribed cutting off the lips of a person who kissed another without permission. The Assyrian code stipulated that if one rapes a virgin, the virgin's father may in turn rape the rapist's wife. The Old Testament avoids two other features of Hammurabi's code: communal responsibility by kin for an individual's acts of crime, and compensation to victims of crime by money. In the Biblical account of Cain and Abel the divine penalty of exile from society notably falls on Cain alone and not collectively on his family. In view of the divine image bestowed on humankind, moreover, Hebrew law sharply distinguished crimes against human life and those against property. The non-Biblical religions, by contrast, permitted monetary compensation for both, as later the Koran did also. The Bible places human life—including that of the stranger—beyond monetary valuation.

II. HUMAN RIGHTS IN THE MEDIEVAL ERA

The human rights tradition that emerged in the West, while deeply rooted in the Bible, was nurtured and shaped also by Athenian democracy and Roman jurisprudence. While all these traditions viewed corporate society as answerable to Deity, they somewhat diversely conceived that relationship.

Greek and Roman sages held that deity is immediately accessible to human reason. Against any such virtual deification of human theoretical activity, the Christian philosopher Augustine emphasized the boundary between Creator and creation and rejected any implication that man's finite and fallen autonomous thought can elaborate truth and the good independently of divine revelation.

Medieval scholasticism nonetheless "Christianized" natural law theory, which rests on the assumption that human reasoning, apart from divine disclosure, can identify a normative objective moral order. Thomas Aquinas held that public reason, independently of revelation, recognizes a "natural law" manifest in the cosmic order and in human nature. To be sure, Thomas attributed natural law to the will of God. He believed that the divine reason, focused on creation, anchored natural law in cosmic law, although Aristotle had viewed natural law as immanent in natural substances.

Beyond its derailment of special revelation, what further distinguished medieval natural-law theory from the evangelical belief in a surviving creational ethic was its insistence that a universally shared body of law and ethics survives the Fall as a present possession of humankind.

The marginality of revelation led to a secularizing of natural-law theory. In consequence, the validity of natural law was championed independently of any divine referent and solely on a foundation of human rationalistic determination.

The Dutch jurist Hugo Grotius (1538) was the watershed. Grotius deduced natural law not from the divine mind or will, nor from a doctrine of creation, but from the human community. He held a universal natural law to be self-evident and so unalterable that not even God could change it and, in fact, discernible independently of God's existence and will. The will of autonomous individuals who constitute a participatory community now replaced an organic society bound by transcendentally stipulated duties and rights. Creative human personality becomes the source of law and rights. Grotius was the founder of the humanistic natural-law theory that dominated Western legal and political thought until early in the nineteenth century, when the historical school of law emerged.

The several philosophical sources contributory to the emphasis on natural morality and natural law—Platonism, Aristotelianism, and Stoicism especially—not only exhibited rival metaphysical assumptions, but they also differed somewhat over the intellectual content of natural ethics and natural law. Medieval scholasticism leaned surreptitiously on the Biblical view in its analysis of human nature, but modern philosophy differed as much over the nature of humanity as it did over the nature of deity. The content of natural morality charted by the several natural-law schools did not wholly agree. Even if consensus had characterized the expositions, such consensus would not in and of itself have established transcendent validity.

The merit of natural-law theory lay in its insistence that positive law has a foundation deeper than the will of the sovereign or of the legislature, that a higher law is regulative of positive law, and in its consequent exclusion of merely subjective, cultural, or evolutionary explanations of law. There was indeed no need to overcredit naturalistic anthropologists who held that for virtually every moral or legal precept they could exhibit a contradictory imperative from another culture. No doubt a sinful race has somewhere corrupted every ethical standard. But such corruptions should not be promptly heralded as reflecting a normative view of morality. Nonetheless, the weakness of natural-law theory remained; without appeal to revelation, and simply by analysis of cosmic order or human nature, it claimed to adduce a universally shared content of morality and law that critics could not really locate.

Grotius and his followers consider humanity no longer subject to transcendent divine law. Speculative natural law has an immanentistic basis, and controls relationships between individuals and between states, although international law is held to rest solely on a contractual agreement between states. No metaphysical order of law, but only the theoretical idea of law, here serves as natural law.

III. HUMAN RIGHTS IN MODERN PERSPECTIVE

Recent modern efforts to revive a theological theory of natural law, mainly by neo-Thomists, remain defensive in posture. After World War II, the theory was vigorously invoked to affirm basic rights, civil liberty and equality, in judgment upon arbitrary Nazi positive law and its accommodation of shifting social conceptualities. Not surprisingly, positivist-analytic and empirico-naturalistic philosophers simply dismiss the view as ideological, as they do all versions of rights-theory that champion valid ethical norms. More importantly, the effort to exhibit rights only through an appeal to human nature, as necessary to the ideal community, or as essential to the concept of human justice, remains the vulnerable point. The attempt to distill a natural-law content from the general consciousness of humanity, independent of revelation, was secretly infused by a prior metaphysical theory. Without some explicit appeal to revelational theism and its conceptual supports, it is difficult to cope with those who see rights only as an evolutionary development of moral conscience or only in terms of majority consensus.

Humanist natural-law thinkers often begin with abstract and equal individuals without authoritative relationships and explain governmental authority over human beings by social contract. Here natural law is stripped of universal normativity; the state is no longer grounded in the organic nature of humanity, let alone considered a divinely-willed instrument for justice, and civil legislation becomes definitive. The fact that certain juridical procedures may have their basis in social contract, however, does not constitute social contract the only referent, or the decisive referent, for civil government. The ahistorical pursuit of ideal law withered under attack by the nineteenth-century historical school which absolutized state legislation as the exclusive source of positive law and its validity. Legal positivism not only rejected any supernatural or natural foundation of the formation and development of law, but it also connected positive law only with the will of the legislator. Here positive law becomes totally variable and arbitrary; validity depends not on material legal principles but on formal-legal approval.

In *Major Trends in the History of Legal Philosophy*,[6] H. J. van Eikema Hommes surveys the proliferating and competing schools of legal theory—sociological, neo-positivist, realist-practical, existential and others—among aggressive naturalistic schools that are dominated by Marx and Engels.[7] In the multiplying rival viewpoints van Eikema Hommes finds evidence of a conceptual instability traceable to the loss of objective transcendent anchorage for law. John Warwick Montgomery emphasizes that none of the seven most influential contemporary philosophies of rights can, with logical consistency, uphold human dignity.[8] Montgomery echoes Alan R. White's complaint that the basis for rights adduced by current theories is cognitively deficient.[9] The naturalistic fallacy—the vain effort to rise from descriptions of what *is* to the identification of an obligatory *ought*—still haunts contemporary theory. Neither updated versions of utilitarianism, H. L. A. Hart's and Hans Kelsen's legal positivism, Ronald Dworkin's legal realism, Julius Stone's quasi-absolutes, John Rawls' and Alan Gewirth's emphasis on prudential rights, nor neo-Kantian nor Marxist theories, Montgomery argues, do or can sustain a genuine *ought*. Legal theory, he affirms, currently confronts us with a plethora of domestic and international rights-claims "with no underlying justification of the purported entitlements other than their embodiment, to varying degrees, in conventions, constitutions, and other instruments of positive law."[10]

Current legal theory therefore leaves in doubt not simply the identification of legitimate rights—a subject that currently preoccupies most juridical controversy—but a clear view also of what, if anything, constitutes legitimacy other than formal-legal validity. The very definition of the concept of law today remains in dispute fully as much as two centuries ago when Kant, in a footnote to his *Critique of Pure Reason* (B759), called for a radical transcendental critique of legal-philosophical thought to exhibit its foundations beyond empirical-inductive observation.

Max L. Stackhouse presses the point that an effective case for rights necessarily rests on metaphysical assumptions.[11] He explores the role of rights in Christianity, Marxism and Hinduism as mirrored in the United States, East Germany and India under Indira Gandhi. All these traditions make universal claims. Stackhouse is not content with mere phenomeno-logical analysis; he contends that the Judeo-Christian tradition best supports universal rights: " . . . to hold and maintain a human rights position that is in principle universal it is necessary to affirm something like the doctrines, and to construct something like those social patterns developed historically by prophetic Judaism, Conciliar Catholicism, Free Church Calvinism, and the principled-liberal tradition. . . ."

Stackhouse's internal criticisms of Hindu and Marxist metaphysics are telling. The American view of rights, moreover, doubtless reflects the contributory channels he indicates, including some accommodation of natural-law theory by the nation's charter political documents. But contemporary liberal-ecumenical discussions tend unfortunately to gloss over the ultimate legitimation of rights and the priority of duties for a Christian view and present no compelling doctrine of divine revelation.

Largely the achievement of John Foster Dulles, the U.N. Declaration of Human Rights skirts the question of the transcendent source and sanction of rights. It remains open, therefore, to the perversion that a superstate might itself finally fill that role. However significant are the stipulated rights for the contemporary cultural crisis, the failure to identify an enforcing agency reduces them to little more than energetic recommendations of universally approved conventions.

IV. HUMAN RIGHTS IN SEARCH OF TRANSCENDENCE

When Kant saw the need two hundred years ago for a radical critique of modern legal theory, one that would exhibit the transcendental foundations of law, he and his followers unfortunately halted short of a recovery of the theistic grounding of law. While they rejected an empirical-inductive foundation, they perpetuated the autonomy of human theoretical thought. The result was that legal theorists routinely fell off the ladder that they thrust into the sphere of the transcendental, since it had no firm divine resting-place. No revelatory basis was acknowledged from which the content of an objectively authoritative morality and law could be derived.

Modern theorists therefore continued to detach human rights from equivalent attention to duties, not to speak of the priority of duty and of God as its basic referent and specifier. The rights of humanity were the main concern; God and duty were marginal. Neo-Kantians had tried to revive duty apart from God, and Kant himself declared that only what is done out of sense of duty is moral, but the genuine objectivity and transcendent authority of the right was nonetheless obscured.

Some natural-law theorists encourage the misconception that all who reject natural law are legal positivists who hold positive law to be the only law. But another great philosophical-theological alternative holds that positive law stands in relationship to transcendent reality and principles without which positive law cannot properly be called law. That alternative is the Augustinian-Calvinistic-Lutheran tradition which emphasizes that universal revelation remains operative but, in contrast to the Thomistic view, affirms that the existential response of a spiritually rebellious humanity conditions human reception of its content. Although no human being is without the light of general revelation, given both externally and internally, the law of God does not survive as a universally shared body of belief. Revelatory Scripture objectively and normatively illumines the now existentially-clouded universal disclosure. The Decalogue summarizes the normative content of law which, contrary to natural-law theory, cannot in humanity's condition of spiritual revolt be comprehensively and universally extracted from the cosmos or from human nature.

Although Calvin used the term "natural law," he did not mean by it "law founded in a metaphysical natural order, valid per se," but rather, as van Eikema Hommes says, the reflection of an original endowment of human nature which, despite its perversion by sin, nonetheless survives as by common grace.[12] Luther likewise conceives of natural law not as "the basis for a specific ethics with theoretically determined maxims" and knowable independently of Scripture. The Reformers dealt more profoundly than did natural-law theorists with the sinful conditions of human nature. The conception of a universally shared supra-positive body of valid legal norms is thus canceled. The intention, however, is not to bestow upon the state creative competence to originate law. For positive law enacted by the state gains normative force and material legal validity as law by incorporating constitutive elements of general revelation that the Scriptural witness objectively focuses, beginning with human dignity and equality that the divine creational image establishes. By no means does this imply that humankind apart from Scripture has no light whatever. But reflection of human dignity, equality, and liberty is here not pursued as if these qualities were inherent in human nature per se, but in the context rather of the will of the transcendent Creator made known in His revelation and correlating rights with the priority of duties to God and humanity.

By no means does affirming the indispensability of Biblical revelation require a contemporary restoration of Hebrew theocracy. The theocracy was a feature of Yahweh's exclusive covenant with Israel for a special purpose. It was annulled by the disobedience, exile and dispersal of the Hebrews, who lost their land; even regathered Jewry now has a secular state. The New Testament abrogates the national and ceremonial legislation of the Old. In the New Testament, Christians are divinely scattered worldwide to witness under many forms of government and in pluralistic societies to the blessings of obedience to the self-revealed Creator and Lord.[13]

In the Christian view, inalienable rights are creational rights governing the community and individual, rights implicit in the social commandments of the Decalogue. The modern separation of rights from duties and from a divine ground encourages a ready misidentification of human needs as rights,[14] since empirical observation of human nature yields conflicting versions of what is "natural" to humanity.

In *A New Critique of Theoretical Thought*,[15] the Dutch scholar Herman Dooyeweerd presses beyond Kant's transcendentalism and seeks a renewal of legal philosophy through a recognition of the God-created order of temporal world structures and life. Dooyeweerd sets juridical meaning structure anew in the Biblical context of creation and fall and redemption, and expounds human existence in cosmonomic frameworks accommodating the positivization of normative principles into valid law. Although Dooyeweerd's cosmonomic categories are not beyond some dispute, he lifts the rights debate above both subjective and natural-law theories through a revival of revelatory theism.

The essentials of this view are summarized by van Eikema Hommes[16] and developed by him in several Dutch works.[17]

However offensive to secular humanists, the theological referent gains double relevance through the conspicuous collapse of modern rights theories. It invests law with transcendent awe and objective authority, and it corresponds to the human condition through its explanation of the confusion over law's nature and content by the fact of moral rebellion. Carl J. Friedrich reminds us that it is not pagan antiquity but specifically Christian belief that undergirds Western constitutionalism's conviction of the dignity and worth of human persons.[18] Jerome Shestack writes: "The concept of a human being created in the image of God certainly endows men and women with a worth and dignity from which there can logically flow the components of a comprehensive human rights system."[19] D. L. Perrott writes: "If it were granted, for the sake of argument, that . . . God does in fact exist, . . . there would be no particular logical difficulty about conceiving His instructions to be highly specific. . . ."[20]

Much as the case for the existence of the God of creation and redemption and judgment may have lost its hold in an empirically-minded century, it has not been disproved. A society that no longer can justify its lofty claims for human rights can ill afford to neglect a rationale that at one and the same time thrusts absolute human rights upon us and makes their observance a test of obedience to the Creator.

John H. Hallowell concludes his *Main Currents in Modern Political Thought*[21] with a penetrating warning: "Having lost sight of the fact that God created all men in His image, . . . the modern world has no basis for believing that all men *are* equal." We are left, he adds, "without any rational means of defending" the belief in individual equality.[22] "The crisis in which we find ourselves," he continues, ". . . is the culmination of modern man's progressive attempt to deny the existence of a transcendent or spiritual reality and of his progressive failure to find meaning and salvation in some wholly immanent conception of reality." The solution lies, he concludes, in the return to "a society that intellectually and spiritually was God-centered rather than man-centered."[23]

The decision over the transcendent authority and objective validity of law and human rights is at one and the same time a decision concerning Biblical theism. No doubt some other religions and philosophies make universal rights claims, all the more as Biblical vitalities impinge upon them. But an unrevealed God is intellectually a cipher, and speculative metaphysical supports are too flimsy to endure. God who reveals Himself, the Judeo-Christian heritage affirms, is the transcendent sovereign; His divine command and stipulation of human duty implies and shelters human rights;[24] His Word particularizes the content of rights beyond mere formal principles and general ethical ideals; His image in humankind constitutes the dignity and value of human life; His judgment of humanity and the nations provides motivation to do the right, and His spiritual empowerment of the penitent supplies a dynamic for performing it; His supreme manifestation in Jesus Christ, "the Just and Holy One," publishes godliness in the flesh and exposes by His crucifixion and resurrection the colossal potentiality for injustice even in a world law-and-order empire that loses touch with the living God.

PART SIX:

BEFORE HELL
BREAKS OUT

SEVENTEEN

THE UNEASY CONSCIENCE REVISITED

Forty years ago—at the unmellowed age of thirty-four—I wrote an eighty-nine-page book titled *The Uneasy Conscience of Modern Fundamentalism*. It appeared in 1947, a few months before Fuller Theological Seminary was founded and two years before Billy Graham's evangelistic crusade in Los Angeles exploded into national headlines.

Looking back, two things sometimes surprise me about *Uneasy Conscience:* how little I said, and how boldly I said it. Sometimes I'm surprised also by how well I said some things that needed urgently to be said. In the 1980s, of course, nothing any longer surprises us about what professing evangelicals and fundamentalists say about each other or, for that matter, what they say about anything. All the more, I appreciate this special opportunity of sharing some septuagenarian reflections.

In 1976 *Newsweek's* cover story heralded The Year of the Evangelical. Its designation of fifty million Americans as born again marked the peaking of a movement that had slowly emerged from its cultural ghetto through incentives like the Graham crusades, the founding of Fuller, and the launching of *Christianity Today* as a thought journal. Those events coalesced in a transdenominational alliance of evangelical theology, evangelism, and social concern that impacted on the church world and the larger culture and helped reshape the face of American Protestantism. *Time* magazine conceded that *Christianity Today's* doctrinal thrust reflected more than a Bible-belt theology; it represented a noteworthy international and interdenominational evangelical scholarship. In a doctoral dissertation at Vanderbilt University,

Larry Sharpe identified this evangelistic, theological and literary coalescence as the high-tide of American evangelicalism.

Today, more than ten years after *Newsweek*'s dramatic cover story, the public media and secular society often depict the evangelical movement in an Elmer Gantry-style of religious exploitation and manipulation.

The culture context that now envelops evangelical Christianity differs markedly from that of forty-plus years ago and bombards evangelicals with critical new challenges. For the moment I merely mention the unmistakable reemergence of paganism in the West; the continuing growth and power of political atheism; the sinkage of secular humanism into raw naturalism; the erosion of general knowledge of cardinal Christian beliefs and the decline of public perception of their plausibility; the scrambling of world religions that nurtures skepticism about the finality of any and every religious faith. But before I suggest some contemporary countermoves let me reach back more than forty years to when evangelicals were still a beleaguered minority—straining to break out of their cultural ghetto, firming their identity against both modernism and neo-orthodoxy, and struggling for academic acceptance and literary achievement.

I

Uneasy Conscience was not an angry diatribe against fundamentalism. What it voiced, rather, was a conscience troubled by the failure of American Christianity to relate Biblical verities to crucial contemporary concerns. By the early 1930s, modernist political theology ruled mainline denominations and many of the churches. A worldling was more likely to learn about the need and possibility of a personal relationship to Jesus Christ, as I did, outside the large churches than through what passed for pulpit proclamation. I was a Long Island newspaper reporter and editor when my Christian conversion occurred in 1933. Fourteen years later, when I wrote *Uneasy Conscience,* I held a doctorate in theology, had taught seminary and college courses in philosophy, theology and ethics, and virtually from its beginnings had been active in the National Association of Evangelicals. Instead of being a newspaperman, I was now a young theologian trying to relate implications of the gospel to students in Chicago and suburban Wheaton; I became increasingly uneasy about the gulf that yawned between evangelical witness and the larger world.

Fundamentalists were devoting their best energies to unmasking the theological defects of Protestant liberalism—its empirical disavowal of miracle, its optimistic hangover-notions of inevitable progress and of man's intrinsic goodness. Their usual approach was to scorn modernist efforts for a new social order. Fundamentalism as such sponsored no program of attack on acknowledged societal evils and ignored serious reflection on how an evangelical ecumenism might impinge on the culture crisis. Even evangelical campuses seemed but remotely aware of crucial world concerns. Intensification of evangelism per se was deemed the solution to every problem.

Fundamentalism, I wrote, did not challenge "the injustices of the totalitarianisms, the secularisms of modern education, the evils of racial hatred, the wrongs of current labor-management relations, the inadequate basis of international dealings" *(Uneasy Conscience,* p. 45). Yet the Kingdom-view of the early Christians, I stressed, in no way frustrated their zeal to challenge and change the world. The Protestant Reformers as well, I noted, had deeper world-concerns than did fundamentalism. "An assault on global evils," I wrote, "is not only consistent with, but rather is demanded by a proper world-life view. . . . If Protestant orthodoxy holds itself aloof from the present world predicament it is doomed to a much reduced role." The startling situation had come to prevail, I lamented, whereby Biblical Christianity, which had historically been the taproot of legitimate public concerns, was now often seen to be undevoted to human well-being. Christianity ought to be in the forefront of social reform by challenging social injustice, political humanism, and evils such as racial intolerance and the liquor traffic. We must oppose all moral evils, societal and personal, and point a better way.

I had no inclination whatever to commend the modernist agenda, for its soft and sentimental theology could not sustain its "millennial fanaticism." Discarding historic doctrinal convictions and moving in the direction of liberalism would not revitalize evangelicalism. Fundamentalism had a realistic view of man and an awareness of the dread cancer of sin. Only supernatural regeneration, I insisted, was adequate to cope with human wickedness.

Essential to Christian ethics, moreover, was the God of the Bible and Scripture as revelation lighting the way to Jesus Christ as Redeemer of mankind.

To applaud communism as the way to utopia or to identify socialism as Christian economics I considered misguided and even wicked. Any controlled society predicated on political omnicompetence has a dark future. No economic organization, capitalism included, is identical with the Kingdom of God. Yet I believed in 1947, as I believe now, in the compatibility of responsible free enterprise with Christianity, although merely utilitarian and libertarian arguments for a market economy are defective.

Forty years ago fundamentalist ethics was largely a catalogue of personal negations (e.g., "Don't smoke," "Don't drink," "Don't gamble," "Don't patronize Hollywood film-fare"), though by hindsight one must now concede that what then often seemed to impinge on individual liberty today has prudence on its side. What I protested was the illogicality of isolating personal ethics from social concerns. Rejecting the illusion of an earthly political utopia should not mean surrendering all interest in sociocultural affairs. Evangelicals needed to discard whatever in their thinking decimated world compassion, needed to revive the global relevance of their redemptive message, to formulate an evangelical social consensus. Their eschatology needed to motivate, not dissipate, cultural concerns. To be sure, the world crisis is not basically political, economic or social, but religious and moral, and only Christ's redemptive dynamic is able to activate humanity to the highest levels of ethical achievement. To press God's claim upon the masses, regenerate Christians must confront the world *now* "with an ethics to make it tremble, and with a dynamic to give it hope." We must offer a new evangelical world-mind whose political, economic, sociological and educational affirmations reflect the Christian world-life view. We must reach for "a baptism of Pentecostal fire resulting in a world missionary program."

The plea for "a divinely empowered Christian community" that would "turn the uneasy conscience of modern evangelicalism into a new reformation," as I put it (p. 88ff.), seemed almost prophetic. Two years later occurred the dramatic breakthrough of the Graham crusades that in time accelerated evangelical evangelism worldwide. Within thirty years the evangelical New Society in the United States alone embraced some fifty million Americans who professed to be "born again."

There was, for all that, a notable weakness in my concentration on regeneration as the guarantee of a better world. For *Uneasy Conscience* failed to focus sharply on the indispensable role of government in preserving justice in a fallen society. Essential as regenerative forces are to transform the human will, civil government remains nonetheless a necessary instrument to constrain human beings—whatever their religious predilections—to act justly, whether they desire to do so or not. At mid-century, in view of assertive totalitarian absolutism in Soviet-sphere countries, I was prone, like evangelicals generally, to emphasize the rightful limits of government. In the context of the American evangelical resurgence, I was prone to minimize the role of law in society and to exalt regeneration in view of its sensitizing of conscience and life-transforming power.

Although redemptive vitalities in society continued to have priority in my thinking, seminars on social ethics during my ten years at Fuller and later showed an enlarging emphasis on the state's mandate for preserving public justice. Among other things, erupting racial tensions underscored civil government's responsibility both for law and order and for nondiscriminatory justice. *Christianity Today,* of which I became founding editor in 1956, from its outset was firmly committed to racial equality. To be sure, we protested massive public demonstrations in defiance of statutory law at a time when respect for law and order was already at low ebb. We favored reliance on legislation and the courts rather than on public demonstrations for social justice. I personally wrote Lyndon Johnson heralding his signing of civil rights legislation as his finest hour in the White House. Yet it was not as painful or reprehensible to us as it should have been that, despite all the operative forces of regeneration, Christians in the Bible belt and elsewhere were largely committed to the *status quo*. We conservatives expected more from evangelical evangelism, and from evangelical sanctification as well, than these vitalities were able to deliver, and many of us underestimated the indispensable importance of legislative coercion in a fallen society. Even at its best, of course, statute law does not impart moral power, but rather compels obedience under threat of penalty. But if law lacks moral force in public life it is not because regenerative powers cancel it, but because secular society has lost sight of law's revelatory foundation and heritage.

Were all humans angels, said James Madison, we wouldn't

need a government. More and more it was evident that American evangelicals lack angelic credentials, much as they profess to side with the heavenly hosts. Having emerged from their subcultural cocoon, evangelicals now are often politically and culturally engaged in ways no less troublesome than their earlier disengagement. To their credit, many evangelicals today pursue careers in political science and law; some have been elected to congressional seats and to governorships, and on occasion an evangelical occupies even the Oval Office. The religious right champions legislative particularities with a zest that had long been the sole prerogative of the ecumenical left. For all that, however, the fastest-growing segment of American Protestantism seems step by step to be forfeiting its major opportunities.

II

I have never considered *Uneasy Conscience* to be a divinely dictated blueprint for evangelical utopia. But I remain troubled that even at a distance of forty years and more some of its challenges remain unheeded.

One of these is the plea for evangelical unity. Evangelical cooperation still lags both outside, inside, and even between the divergent ecumenical and/or nonecumenical alignments. It is superficial to say—and I too have said it—that despite the evangelical insistence that true church unity is impossible apart from doctrinal consensus, pluralistic ecumenism reflects more church unity than does the conservative movement. The fact is that in 1900 there were under two thousand denominations and only one multidenominational council, namely the World Evangelical Alliance. Since then the twentieth-century pursuit of an ecumenical world church is faced by forty-five world confessional councils, three international councils of churches, and more than twenty thousand denominations. In the United States many evangelical churches remain outside the National Association of Evangelicals and amble along with the National Council of Churches. Some N.C.C.-affiliated evangelicals welcome Mark Ellingsen's call in *The Evangelical Movement: Growth, Impact, Controversy and Dialogue* (Augsburg, 1988) for a deliberate influx of conservatives to challenge ecumenism's theological pluralism and relativistic hermeneutic (cf. C. F. H. Henry, "Where Will Evangelicals Cast their

Lot?," *This World,* Summer 1987, pp. 3-11; chapter 10 of this book). His appeal especially attracts those who because of qualified views of Biblical reliability are set off from the evangelical mainline. At the same time, numbers of active evangelical churches continue their exodus from ecumenical association into newly established Reformed, Wesleyan, or other transdenominational configurations.

Another major call in *Uneasy Conscience* was for evangelical academic and literary engagement. Sounding a warning that "secular education largely involves an open or subtle undermining of historic Christian theism," *Uneasy Conscience* pleaded for quality literature from elementary through university levels. The remarkable gains in this area during my generation have been gratifying. No one should undervalue the cognitive contributions of Fuller Seminary, Trinity Evangelical Divinity School, Gordon-Conwell Theological Seminary and other schools, *Christianity Today* and other magazines, as well as the Institute for Advanced Christian Studies and other agencies. Conservative theological and philosophical literature rivals the evangelical material of the pre-modernist era a century ago. Emergence of the Society of Christian Philosophers within the orbit of the American Philosophical Association has placed supernatural theism once again on the speculative agenda of professional philosophers.

Secular humanism nonetheless remains the masked metaphysics of Western university learning. Its disbelief in supernatural realities undermines the credal affirmations that evangelical orthodoxy trumpets to the world. The Chicago philosopher Allan Bloom traces much of today's cognitive and ethical confusion to present-day university education; academe impoverishes rather than enriches and illumines young people, he protests. All too few students any longer wrestle the questions of what is good, what is true, what is man. Relativism is the dominant force on campuses, Bloom contends, and has corrupted the university mind. Despite national consensus on the urgent need for shared values, less and less agreement exists on which values to champion and why. The only virtue now highly respected on many campuses, Bloom comments, is openness. Market demand is what decides the importance and composition of school curricula. Personal and interpersonal commitments have little permanence; marriage is considered expendable, and sex becomes as routine as going to a shopping mall. The contemporary crisis is philosophical, Bloom stresses.

The self has displaced the soul, values have replaced right and wrong, openness and autonomy have eroded authority. In short, modern man has become "spiritually detumescent."

High schools and elementary schools are increasingly being sucked into this secular tailwind. Textbook controversies are often settled by an openness to all religious faiths and the delegation of theistic belief to myth. Yet the American Constitution was not written by atheists; the Founding Fathers championed public interest in morality and religion as essential to a democracy, and they derived inalienable human rights from the supernatural Creator. But classrooms today avoid descriptive references to religion and suspend moral standards. Peter Berger is right; modernity, he says, is "a great relativizing caldron" and the interplay of external cultural forces with subjective beliefs yields nothing less than a relativization of all worldviews.[1] The secularized modern consciousness shapes "an unparalleled pluralization of meanings and values."[2]

Meanwhile, secular humanism is drawn into irresistible concessions to uncompromising naturalism. Evangelical theists on the right and thoroughgoing naturalists on the left both declare the social imperatives of humanism to be powerless since it denies that personality and truth and morality are ultimate and fixed. University students indoctrinated in the notion that reality reduces finally to impersonal processes and energy events find no reason for affirming transcendentally-binding ethical imperatives.

The skeptical pressure that naturalism exerts on any moral agenda was blatantly evident when President Frank Rhodes of Cornell University suggested to a Harvard audience that the nation's academic centers need seriously to attend to the "intellectual and moral well-being" of students. Catcalls from both faculty and students interrupted the address, and applause greeted one heckler's inquiry as to just who would provide moral instruction for others and whose morality would be promoted.

The loss of divine-command morality has eroded the transcendent ethical foundations of behavior. As G. E. M. Anscombe warns, if obligation statements are to make any sense, morality must be recoupled with a divine-law conception of ethics.[3] Atheism forfeits the resources that sustain even the tattered remnants of morality because it strips right and wrong of their transcendent and objective authority.

American evangelicals unfortunately never established a national Christian university in a great metropolitan center. That forfeited opportunity is even now only partially compensated for by countermoves on the edge of influential secular campuses. Even leading evangelical seminaries and colleges have experienced a dilution of consistent orthodoxy. This fact prompts James H. Hunter to ask just how effectively these institutions any longer present a cohesive Christian world-life view to their students.[4] In its largest dimensions, therefore, the conflict today between theistic and naturalistic learning is even more acute than forty years ago.

Evangelical imperatives reach far beyond concerns of church unity and academic engagement, however. When *Newsweek* a decade ago depicted burgeoning evangelicalism, it noted emerging subsurface trouble spots such as tensions over Biblical authority, over the nature and direction of social activism and public involvement, and over an exuberant health-and-wealth theology that shuns a lifestyle marked by sacrifice and perhaps even suffering. Also noted was evangelicalism's lack of a precise philosophy of cultural engagement and the marked distancing of Southern Baptist leadership and professors from evangelical identification. Was the evangelical movement then in danger of being held together less by doctrinal and intellectual coherence than by a confluence of tradition and inner experience, not to mention computerized mailings and pungent one-liners by media evangelists?

During the past decade, *Newsweek*'s prognosis erupted into major evangelical afflictions. What N.A.E. at its founding in 1942, Fuller at its founding in 1947, and *Christianity Today* at its founding in 1956 envisioned as a cohesive theological and social thrust had become so diversified in less than a generation that some of us began to press the question of evangelical identity (cf. C. F. H. Henry, *Evangelicals in Search of Identity,* Waco, TX: Word, 1976). Founders of these enterprises would have viewed defection from the Bible's unqualified authority as a hermeneutical shift of grave consequences for formulating Christian theology and ethics. Precisely at the time that evangelicalism's life-transforming dynamic confronted American society on an unprecedented scale with a demand for moral and spiritual decision, evangelicals themselves divided publicly over the issue of Biblical authority.

The other public window on evangelicalism was its aggressive move into sociopolitical affairs. Conservatives were provoked into public involvement by federal intrusion into areas of moral and religious concern such as funding of abortions and prohibition of prayer in public schools. Devoid of a comprehensive political philosophy, evangelicals as individuals or groups tended to be confrontational and single-issue oriented. Reentry into the public arena often lent itself to exploitation by entrepreneurial and charismatic leaders who sought media visibility, financial support, and even political influence or political office. Although the religious right was unable to secure passage of a single legislative proposal, it nonetheless became significantly influential in other ways, even if no comprehensive evangelical consensus emerged.

What eluded evangelical leadership in this reach for political influence and power was the extent to which American evangelicalism was being swamped by the very culture that it sought to alter. The question of evangelical identity shifted from differences over Biblical authority and over political agenda to the very definition of evangelical selfhood. Evangelical self-understanding and evangelical social identity have undergone remarkable changes. A generation ago evangelicals by and large considered world-renunciation a mark of regeneration and disdained so-called worldly pleasures. Many young evangelicals have emancipated themselves from the traditional "*don't*s." But, as Hunter observes, the striking fact is that "no new prohibitions are replacing the old ones."[5] Some young evangelicals now define sin almost entirely in terms of social injustice. Premarital sex is common. Church discipline is lax or nonexistent. Divorce and remarriage snares even the clergy. The idea that spiritual and moral foundations are basic and essential for successful home life seems passé. Society's preoccupation with physical satisfactions has invaded much evangelical thinking and practice.

More than this, Hunter finds that the new generation of evangelicals is overturning the traditional perception of "the nature and value of the self."[6] While evangelicals reject "unbiblical Narcissism," there is little remorse for the sinful self; prime concern centers, rather, on self-potential, self-fulfillment, and even self-veneration. No clear line is drawn between self-indulgence and self-affirmation. Many seem unaware that the modern self-fulfillment cults are really, as Paul Vitz notes, a form of self-worship under the guise of humanist self-esteem. Selfism elevates the subjective ego to ultimacy, to the idolatrous worship of one's own selfhood.[7] Daniel Yankelovich reminds us: "the Christian

172

injunction that to find one's self one must first lose one's self contains an essential truth any seeker of self-fulfillment needs to grasp."[8] From Sartre's existentialist belief that we make ourselves what we will—that is, the self-created self—the next aberration is not too far distant—namely that what is sacred lies within the self. In that case we are potentially our own objects of worship. Carl Frederick puts it bluntly: "*You* are the supreme being."[9]

The grip of the physical on evangelical life is evident also in its materialistic priorities. Many evangelicals became or were already middle-class during the movement's early years and have capitulated increasingly to the lure of the secular marketplace. Alongside many believers in the Two-Thirds world, almost all American believers are considered rich. In fact, American believers are estimated to have the income and resources to reach the whole earth for Christ. About 80 percent of the world's Christian wealth is presumed to exist in the one hundred and fifty thousand churches in the United States. Yet members of U.S. churches are said on average to give to Christian causes only 2.5 percent of their income—that is, $25 out of every $1,000. Even Southern Baptists, whose vast numbers accommodate one of Christendom's largest missionary programs, average less than $10 per year per communicant for world missions. Think of it—less than it takes for a restaurant meal on bargain night to save a world without Christ, a world of over four billion people, half of whom have yet to hear the gospel. Yet only one in thirty congregations in the United States sends and supports even one of its members in full-time missionary activity elsewhere in the world. Affluence renders us self-indulgent and spiritually myopic, whereas economic privilege ought to enlarge our vision of evangelistic and stewardship opportunities.

Prayerlessness is often the key to this spiritual insensitivity. We may be rich in this world's goods, but spiritual vitality we have not because we ask not. Many evangelical churches have eliminated prayer meetings. Even pulpit prayers on Sunday mornings are sometimes little more than formal invocations. I remember how at Westminster Chapel, London, famous for the preaching of G. Campbell Morgan and Martyn Lloyd-Jones, I was told to take ten to twelve minutes for pulpit prayer before preaching, lest the congregation perceive me as not knowing how to pray.

The secularism we increasingly confront and unfortunately accommodate is the expiring skeleton of humanism that is decomposing into paganism. Much of the secular media disdains inherited values, particularly the Biblical ideals of chastity, marriage and family. Impersonal processes and quantum events are considered ontologically ultimate. As physical and material elements are given priority, man's mind and heart become realigned to idolatrous affections. Even some supposedly Christian theologians forsake the supernatural. "Any viable future Christian philosophy or theology," writes John O. Cooper, "will be a theology that sees the transcendent within this world, for it will be based on a philosophy that recognizes no other world."[10] The hope of immortality succumbs to a desire for immortalism by genetic engineering. The worldview emerging among us, writes Peter Marin, "centers solely on the self" and "individual survival as its sole good."[11]

What paganism is doing to human life—not only to the life of the spirit but to the whole self and to man in society—demands penetrating analysis. What remains of virtue when the human species is considered animal flesh useful for sexual exploitation, profitable for material gain, serviceable for political terrorism? We discuss nuclear war in terms of anticipated body counts, as if humans were so many cows or horses. What has happened to humaneness in a world where some ten million persons have AIDS and the whole human race is imperiled?

American society, in which evangelicalism thrives, is undergoing a catastrophic culture shock. Not only in theory but in practice as well, the rising tide of moral indecency inundates our culture. The devaluation of human life is evident in the millions of abortions and in the increased acceptance and practice of euthanasia. To the trashing of the beginning and end of life we must now add the sad statistics of suicide by disillusioned and despairing young people. On every hand the violation of personal worth and dignity is hastening us to cultural Armageddon.

Television networks that define good programming by audience ratings, Wall Street's accommodation of greedy inside traders, government-sponsored lotteries that foist "get-rich-quick" delusions on low-income families, drug addicts numbering some seventy million, a crime rate second only to that of Beirut, Lebanon, the world's highest divorce rate, a multitude of cohabitating unmarrieds, a million teenage pregnancies annually—are we to shun these realities as patriotic unmentionables, or do we deplore them as disturbing evidence of a nation moving perilously toward sunset, despite a contingent of fifty million evangelicals, all too many of whom, like Lot's wife, may linger for a titillating glimpse of Sodom?

In a society that is losing faith in life itself, the moral integrity and spiritual vitality of Christians—theologians, evangelists and clergy included—is doubly important. The secular city's perception of the clergy and of churches is changing. For many of the unchurched, religion represents only some sort of hypocritical enterprise. As it has always done, the renegade spirit justifies its distance from spiritual commitment by pointing accusatory fingers at dark chapters in religious life and history; it fails to discern that even the moral judgments it levels against others reflect Christian criteria that summon all mankind to Christ the sinless Savior. The day has come when local churches, whose congregations are known by upright lives and neighbor-love, are once again decisively important witnesses to Christ and His Kingdom.

Meantime, American society is being penetrated as never before by alien religious influences that the West unhesitatingly once called pagan. Even witchcraft is practiced much as in pre-Christian societies; demonism and satanic cults are likewise on the increase. Various forms of oriental religions call harried and affluent Westerners to quiet meditation and self-denial. Refugees and immigrants from around the world have given new prominence to assorted religious practices. Mosques, shrines and temples now dot our cities alongside the more traditional worship centers.

This development faces American evangelicalism in new depth with the issues of religious liberty and of inter-religious confrontation. America's humanitarian welcome to thousands of non-Christians at a time when her public institutions are already permeated by secular humanism no doubt further dilutes the cohesiveness of Judeo-Christian influences. Yet the first test of a good evangelical conscience under God is commitment to religious liberty not for Christians only but for all human beings. If evangelicals have learned well the lessons of history, they know that genuine faith thrives best in a context of voluntary religion and that state religion is as costly to the religious community as it is to government. To guarantee freedom of religious preference to others underscores the importance of a voluntary faith, including the right to change one's religion without penalty. This is especially significant where and when some cultures still disown, disinherit and even maim those who forsake their religious tradition. More important still is the fact that God seeks humanity's voluntary spiritual allegiance; coerced decision is of little spiritual value. In the long run religious restriction is just as devastating for revealed religion as it is for pagan religion.

That fact does not, however, imply the impropriety of intrareligious dialogue, cognitive exchange and evangelistic effort. Is it not a fair test of missionary concern whether or not we share the eternal Good News with distant peoples who in God's providence have come to our own shores and communities? We have on our very doorstep an unprecedented missionary opportunity. The evangelical imperative toward non-Christians involves forging constructive contacts by manifesting love and compassion, sharing Biblically-revealed truths, and personally mirroring the vitalities of redemption. To invite explanation of what the Deity in which one professes to believe actually achieves in one's life and outlook can open a conversational door to larger understanding. Even better than the witnessing Christian, a one-time Buddhist, Hindu or Muslim who comes to know the living Christ will be able to explain what God does for him that other gods could not.

The neglect of such involvement will almost surely foster increased paganism. The twentieth century in which evangelicals proposed to win the world for Christ in a single generation has in fact become the age in which religious atheism swept millions of persons into its ranks and in which political atheism now rules half the world's population and much of its landmass.

Naturalism grants Christianity no ontological credentials superior to the legendary and mythological gods of the Babylonians, Greeks or Romans, and no more metaphysical legitimacy than Hinduism or Taoism. In whatever guise it appears, naturalism is the metaphysical nullification of the God of the Bible.

Yet naturalism accommodates three ways of viewing religion-in-general and its collectivity of gods.

Atheistic totalitarianism is one such naturalistic perception of religion, and undoubtedly the most repressive. It regards religion as harmful illusion, an opiate. The gods are traced to human imagination, desire or volition. Any notion that a divine being functions in nature or history is declared a fantasy. Communist nations are prone to restrict religious propaganda unless it can be deployed to reinforce revolutionary politics.

Secular humanism is another form of naturalism. It too grants no ontological status to deity, whether it be the Biblical Yahweh or the Babylonian Marduk. But it is more open than atheistic totalitarianism to a functional role for religion. It attributes the rival religions with internally integrating the perspectival outlook of their followers. It values religion insofar as it supplies cohesive unity to the beleaguered human ego; religion, it says, serves to integrate the outlook and life of the discordant self. Humanism contends, however, that religion falsifies the facts if it ventures to give us substantial data about God or the gods, or presumes to tell us how reality is objectively constituted. Religion is psychologically useful, humanists say, but not substantively true. By thus linking inner personal unity with faith in nonexistent gods, humanism faces the additional difficulty of defining religion in a day when many persons profess to find a unifying perspective through hallucinatory drugs, social protest, or even insider trading on Wall Street.

A third spur of naturalism affirms the divine sanctity of all existence and steeps man in cosmic nature as a spiritual process. Approximating ancient Greek and Roman nature-worship, such neo-pagan naturalism would return us to the pre-Christian cosmic gods. It is equally hostile to materialistic atheism and to Biblical theism; both, it charges, desacralize the cosmos. It freely applauds Hinduism, Buddhism, and African animist religions, but lampoons the Christian creeds as evidence of the West's alienation from reality. The God of the Bible is supplanted by imaginative divinities; a personified cosmos is viewed through the lenses of mystical polytheism. Communion with nature is perceived as humanity's spiritual lifeline, and the joy of being is linked to an intensification of mankind's given existence. What Christians call human unregeneracy this naturalism champions as normal natural life.

A religion of occult forces and powers, on which J. Gordon Melton reports in *Magic, Witchcraft, and Paganism in America,* is but one offshoot of this development. Largely transplanted from Europe, mainly Britain, it includes also some African and Caribbean aspects. Within its larger circle of its devotees, a professional inner group who practice magic "believe in a plurality of deities, the gods and goddesses of pre-Christian polytheism. They revere the earth and the forces of nature and attempt to attune themselves to them."[12] By the early 1980s the American followers of occultism numbered between thirty thousand and forty thousand, many of whom meet in regional or national festivals. They reject both the Christian God and the Christian anti-God, namely Satan. Nature-religion is their stance; they worship Mother Earth and seek to become one with the gods.

Although naturalism assimilates Christianity to religion-in-general, it views it as but one of many cults espousing strange beliefs. In a review of High Milne's book on the Indian guru Rajneesh (*Bhagwan, The God that Failed*, 1982), Grace Lichtenstein remarks that one "might almost say" that the United States was "founded by cultists."[13]

While these cults attack the reality of the Biblical God, many timid Christians hesitate to challenge the reality or worship of non-Biblical gods. What deters them is a growing notion that religious tolerance does not or ought not raise questions about a religion's objective truth. Humanism deplores the Bible's condemnation of alien religions and, like paganism, makes room for them. Paganism champions the inexhaustible fruitfulness of the myths and commends the unprobed riches of what Christians dismiss as works-religions. Temples and mosques become objects of new curiosity; sites are marked where deity is held to be specially present. Local festivals and feasts are opened on holy days for sharing, much as many secular Americans now celebrate Christmas and Easter.

In ancient Greece and Rome the time came when multitudes gathered in temples to revere one or another of the many gods; people thronged cult theatres to hear poetic and hymnodic tributes to their deities; special fairs were associated with different gods. Religion came to pervade all of life. The rich and noble underwrote many a festival and welcomed religion as a social epoxy. The issue was not whether religious sentiment is true, but whether religious feelings are useful. Although ambiguity over life after death voided the topic of immortality, the gods nonetheless were said to reward piety and to punish wickedness in this life. Religion was therefore praised for its social utility. Local varieties of religion became a matter of civic pride and attracted tourists and travelers. Every group and city had its favored deities; even pagan rulers erected statues to their special god or gods, and thus elevated a particular worship. Cult leaders and community officials paid reciprocal honor to each other. The aristocracy testified to the benefits of specific religious preferences; its subsidies supplied housing for the gods and supported temple activities. Even the poor gave offerings or donations. Tourists came for souvenirs, and merchants commercialized artifacts specially suited to specific divinities. Military personnel and others patronized prostitutes, while the fragrance of incense sanctified the whole scene.

At one point statues of various deities seemed almost omnipresent in the Roman Empire. Thought to be specially present in such images, the gods were associated with revelation in dreams, and were considered the source of oracles mediated by priests or by intermediaries. The whole natural order was related to one or another of these divinities. First and foremost the pagans prayed for health; interest in salvation concerned physical well-being more than the soul's eternal felicity.

Throughout the Roman Empire it was wrong to slight the plural gods. Almost everyone had his or her distinctive way of life. Over and above the almost endless variety of cults, civil religion gave shape to holidays or festivals. This loyalty to the gods lent paganism a universal vitality; it had its own feelings and dynamic behavior patterns, and embraced all known religions—with one notable exception, namely Christianity.

This overview suggests links to today's emerging religious pluralism. A leading secular historian, Ramsay MacMullen, observes that such ancient superstition actually "survives today" and in fact "receives attention daily in the newspaper."[14] One might note the localizing of religious interest in terms of civic pride, the emphasis on the social utility of religion, the secular holiday revelry and commercializing of religion, the preoccupation with health more than with the afterlife, the breakdown of sexual morality among religious professionals, and the pluralistic intolerance of absolutistic religious claims. The cross-pollination of religious ideas is reflected in a Gallup report that one in four Americans believes in reincarnation. Some observers think that the politicizing of religious beliefs in America may in time duplicate the European tendency to transfer religious impulses from God to the nation, from God to tradition, from God to culture and art. The wave of the immediate future is not neo-orthodoxy but neo-paganism; rumbling in the near distance is the echo not of Barth but that of Celsus.

For ancient Roman thought the spiritual enemy was atheism, and Christianity was reckoned to be exactly that. In MacMullen's words, "nonatheists were rated as atheists."[15] The reason for such illogic was simple: not to perpetuate all the cults was an offense against divinity; to seek to replace them was disrespectful and intolerant. Roman religion in turn welcomed Yahweh only on polytheistic terms. But since Christianity repudiated idols, disowned nature divinities, and resisted polytheism, it was considered an enemy. Only in the universities was the possibility discussed of there being but one god who worked his will through the many gods as aspects of his absolute divinity manifested in different realms of action. But to Christians even this blend of Stoicism and Neo-Platonism was fully as objectionable as the paganism of the marketplace.

Today the prospect of an upsurge of religious life on a colossal pagan scale is reemerging in the West. It looks as a special possibility in the United States where all contemporary religious contenders maintain a presence.

It is highly probable that in tomorrow's world Christianity will need to fend for itself either in a secularized social milieu of intellectual atheism that empties the churches or in a society where a religious sense of many coexisting gods saturates civic culture as did ancient paganism. In the one case, Christian orthodoxy will be charged with espousing the objective existence of a supernatural reality in an age when religion is presumed to traffic only in optional myths; in the other case, Christian orthodoxy will be charged anew with intolerance and with atheism because to deny everyone else's gods violates public piety and its approval of the plural gods. Robin Lane Fox describes the ancient Roman Empire as a complex milieu in which Christianity emerged not as a refreshing breeze amid stifling atheism, but as an extreme and radical option that offended a regnant religiosity.[16] What began as social disdain for Christians because of their disrespect for other divinities led in turn to the verdict that Christians were dangerous and that their contempt for the plural gods is what precipitated social calamities.

Atheistic secularism may suit many intellectuals who in their leadership posts tend to view themselves as the very essence of reality. The masses, however, apart from an official totalitarian repression of religion, and even in the face of it, are more apt to reflect loyalty to the gods, whatever that implies. Because of the Middle East's Islamic political expansion and the West's religious pluralism, it is unlikely that the totalitarian atheism of Eastern Europe and of China will supply the paradigm for society elsewhere.

Unless Christian scholars affirm the truth of Christianity in the context of public reason, rival religions will not respect its claim to universal truth or consider it worthy of a universal hearing. It is not enough that Biblical theists mount a soapbox in a pluralistic society to declare that evangelicals offer their own unique perspective on life, that the Christian outlook has as much right to representation as do the multiple modern alternatives, and that we shall blow our trumpet as loudly as others because no one any longer can be sure of the right tune. The ancient Romans absorbed to their pantheon one novel deity after another.

Early Christian thinkers did not evade the task of evaluating non-Biblical religions and philosophies. They spoke of humanly manufactured gods, of religious absurdities and irrationalities, of all variety of conflicting interpretations of the divine, of myths of dead and reborn divinities, of gods guilty of adultery and theft. Beyond this they witnessed to the sovereignty and grace of the one true and living God revealed supremely in Jesus Christ, "the only one of the Father's kind." They held a more critical view of paganism's degraded worship and debased practices than most American Christians do today. The church father Lactantius wrote of "religions which are false," whereas today frontier theologians invoke the doctrine of the Logos to upgrade the non-Biblical religions and to insist that they are not without some affirmation of truth.

We must choose to cast our lot either with a society that admits only private faiths, and then simply add another idol to modernity's expanding God-shelf, or we must hoist a banner to a higher Sovereign, the Lord of lords and King of kings. Just as the Christian witness to "one Lord, one faith, one baptism" invited unrelenting persecution by Roman authorities, so also Christianity's reiteration of a universal validity-claim still invites and will continue to invite the entrenched hostility of modern intellectual authority. But our awesome imperative as Christian scholars is to address the divided mind and civilizational turmoil of modernity. The loss of Biblical theism takes its steady toll as world-wisdom declines from theism to humanism and then from humanism to animalism, the neo-paganism of our time.

If evangelicals believe that the enduring corrective of modernity's badly-skewed ethical and epistemic compass is the self-disclosed God and His moral agenda, they had better say so and live so in this crucial turning-time in America. Otherwise they may soon find themselves aliens in a once promised land. We may even now live in the half-generation before hell breaks loose and, if its fury is contained, we will be remembered, if we are remembered at all, as those who used their hands and hearts and minds and very bodies to plug the dikes against impending doom.

NOTES

Chapter 8:
Feed Them on Fantasies

1. *The Economic Review,* Vol. XVIII (1907), p. 199.

Chapter 13:
Christian Fund-Raising Heresies

1. Oriental Missionary Fellowship, with a $5 million domestic and $5 million international budget, still follows J. Hudson Taylor's policy of indicating financial needs only if information is requested.
2. In respect to administrative and trustee functions, Christian institutions have been even more influenced by secular models than in respect to funding, although that theme requires separate discussion. The increasing disposition to operate an essentially spiritual organization on a secular corporation structural model has as many liabilities as assets, and readily accommodates the redefinition of an enterprise's original purpose and mission.
3. The question of acceptance or nonacceptance of federal funds, a subject that falls outside the purview of this discussion, raises many of the same issues and introduces still others.

Chapter 15:
The Christian Scholar's Task in a Stricken World

1. Quoted by Ingo Hermann, "Total Humanism," in Johannes B. Metz, ed., *Is God Dead? Concilium,* Vol. 16 (New York: Paulist Press, 1966), p. 166.
2. Quoted by Richard Shaull, in Carl Oglesby and Richard Shaull, *Containment and Change* (New York: Macmillan, 1969), p. 214.
3. John H. Hallowell, *Main Currents in Modern Political Thought* (New York: Holt, Rinehart and Winston, 1965), p. 627.
4. Review of Willis B. Glover, *Biblical Origins of Modern Secular Culture: An Essay in the Interpretation of Western History* (Macon, GA: Mercer University Press, 1984), *Journal of the American Academy of Religion,* Vol. LIV, No. 2, Summer 1986, p. 375.

5. Thomas Dean, *Post-Theistic Thinking,* The Marxist-Christian Dialogue in Radical Perspective (Philadelphia: Temple University Press, 1975), p. 317.
6. Herman Dooyeweerd, *In the Twilight of Western Thought* (Nutley, NJ: Craig Press, 1965), p. 175.
7. Lesslie Newbigin, *Foolishness to the Greeks,* The Gospel and Western Culture (Grand Rapids: Eerdmans, 1986), p. 14.
8. *Ibid.,* p. 20.
9. Claude Geffré, *A New Age in Theology* (New York: Paulist Press, 1974), p. 60.
10. *Ibid.,* p. 51.
11. Cf. Robert P. Scharlemann, "The Being of God When God Is Not Being God," in Thomas J. J. Altizer, *et al., Deconstruction in Theology* (New York: Crossroad, 1982), p. 80.
12. Max A. Myers, "Toward What Is Religious Thinking Underway?," in *ibid.,* p. 109n.
13. *Ibid.,* p. 140ff.
14. Carl A. Raschke, "The Deconstruction of God," in *ibid.,* pp. 30, 28.
15. *Ibid.,* p. 3.
16. *Ibid.,* p. 109n.
17. Reuben Abel, *Man Is the Measure* (New York: The Free Press, 1976), p. 272ff.
18. Lesslie Newbigin, "Can the West Be Converted?," *International Bulletin of Missionary Research,* Vol. 11, No. 1, January 1987, p. 2.
19. Newbigin, *Foolishness to the Greeks,* p. 65.

Chapter 16:
The Judeo-Christian Heritage and Human Rights

1. "Christianity and Human Rights—A Jurist's Reflections," in Lorenz, ed., *How Christian Are Human Rights?* p. 29.
2. *The Theological Foundations of Law* (Garden City: Doubleday, 1960).
3. *History of Israel* (New York: Harper & Row, 1958), p. 128.
4. *Human Rights in Jewish Law* (New York: KTAV, 1984), p. 17ff.
5. *The Rights of Man Today* (Boulder, CO: Westview Press, 1978), p. 1.
6. New York/Amsterdam: The North-Holland Pub. Co., 1979.
7. In the first generation after the Communist revolution, the most prominent Soviet legal theorist, E. B. Pashu Kanis, held that all law is *bourgeois* and that promotion of *proletarian*-law contravenes Marxism. But Soviet Russia had to abandon the theory that a Communist society would evaporate both the state and law. Later writers defend the necessity of Soviet law, although the theory of state-absolutism assigns it a subservient role.
8. *Human Rights and Human Dignity* (Grand Rapids: Zondervan, 1986), p. 81ff.
9. *Rights* (Oxford: Clarendon, 1984), p. 172ff.
10. *Op. cit.,* p. 106.
11. *Creeds, Society and Human Rights* (Grand Rapids: Eerdmans, 1986).

12. *Op. cit.,* p. 76.
13. While excluding theocracy and religious establishment, the American political charter documents insisted on the Creator's role as the transcendent ground of unalienable rights, including religious freedom. The appeal to natural rights emerged only after extensive colonial political debate. The Stamp Act Congress (1765) appealed not to laws of nature but only to God as a higher authority than the English Parliament. The Declaration and Resolves of the First Continental Congress (1774), however, declared oppressive English measures to be in violation of "the laws of nature." There was long debate—so John Adams later reports—whether such an appeal should be made over and above the principles of the English Constitution and colonial charters and grants. The decision to appeal to nature as a basis of rights influenced the draft of the Declaration of Independence (1776), as it did also the Constitution of Virginia (1776), although these both grounded rights in the Creator.
14. Cf. John Finnis, *Natural Law and Natural Rights* (Oxford: Clarendon Press, 1980).
15. Amsterdam, N. J.; Paris, 1953; Philadelphia: Presbyterian and Reformed Publishing Company, 1958.
16. *Major Trends in the History of Legal Philosophy,* chap. 15.
17. *De elementaire grondbegrippen der rechtswetensschap,* Deventer, Kluwer, 1972; *De samengestelde grondbegrippen der rechtswetensschap,* Zwolle, W. E. J. Tjeenk Willink, 1976.
18. *Transcendent Justice: The Religious Dimensions of Constitutionalism* (Durham, NC: Duke University Press, 1964).
19. "The Jurisprudence of Human Rights," in *Essays on Human Rights* (Philadelphia: Jewish Publication Society of America, 1979), p. 76ff.
20. "The Logic of Fundamental Rights," in J. W. Bridge, D. Lasok, *et al.,* eds., *Fundamental Rights* (London: Sweet and Maxwell, 1973), p. 12.
21. New York: Holt, Rinehart and Winston, 1965.
22. *Ibid.,* p. 627.
23. *Ibid.,* p. 652.
24. Montgomery impressively correlates human rights reflected in the Biblical revelation with those affirmed by the European Convention on Human Rights (1950), and notes that some go beyond the latter *(Human Rights and Human Dignity,* p. 167ff.) Admittedly not exhaustive, Montgomery's list includes procedural due process rights—impartiality of tribunal (Mal. 2:9, 1 Tim. 5:21); fair hearing (Exod. 22:9); prompt trial (Ezra 7:26); confrontation of witnesses (Isa. 43:9); no double jeopardy (Nah. 1:9). Under substantive due process rights he lists nondiscrimination in general (Acts 10:34; Deut. 16:19; Prov. 24:23); equality before the law (Matt. 5:45); racial, sexual and social equality (Gal. 3:28; Amos 9:7; Exod. 21:2); equality of rich and poor (James 2:1-7; Amos 5:12; Isa. 1:16, 17); equality of citizens and foreigners (Exod. 12:47; Lev. 23:22; 24:22; Num. 9:14; 15:15, 16); even the sovereign is subordinate to the law (2 Sam. 11—12). Under miscellaneous basic first-, second-, and third-generation rights he lists right to life (Exod. 20:13; Ps. 51:5; Matt. 5:21, 22; Luke 1:15, 41); right to family life (1 Tim. 5:8); humane treatment and punishment (Luke 6:45); freedom of thought, conscience,

religion, expression, assembly, association, movement (John 7:17); social and economic rights in general (1 Cor. 6:19, 20); right to universal education (Deut. 6:7; 11:19); right to work, fair remuneration and good working conditions (Luke 10:7; 1 Tim. 5:18; Deut 23:25, 26; 24:6, 10, 12-13, 15); right to protection of honor and reputation (Exod. 20:16); right to leisure time (Exod. 20:8-11); right to asylum (Exod. 21:31; Josh. 20; 1 Chron. 6:67; *et al.*); right to equitable distribution of land (Num. 33:54; Lev. 25:14-18, 25-34); and environmental rights. In some cases, though surely not in all, the indicated rights-claims call for firmer Scriptural anchorage and accreditation.

Chapter 17:
The Uneasy Conscience Revisited

1. *The Heretical Imperative* (New York: Anchor Press, Doubleday, 1979), p. 10ff.
2. *Ibid.*, p. 24.
3. "Modern Moral Philosophy," *Philosophy,* 33, January 1958, pp. 1-19.
4. *Evangelicalism, The Coming Generation* (Chicago: University of Chicago Press, 1987).
5. *Ibid.*
6. *Ibid.*, p. 65.
7. *Psychology as Religion: The Cult of Self-Worship* (Grand Rapids: Eerdmans, 1977), p. 93.
8. *New Rules: Searching for Self-Fulfillment in a World Turned Upside Down* (New York: Bantam, 1982), p. 239.
9. *est: Playing the Game the New Way* (New York: Dell, 1974), p. 168ff.
10. *The Roots of Radical Theology* (Philadelphia: Westminster Press, 1967), p. 156ff.
11. Quoted by Christopher Lasch, *The Culture of Narcissism* (New York: W. W. Norton, 1978), p. 6.
12. *Magic, Witchcraft, and Paganism in America* (Garland, 1982), p. 6.
13. "Book World," *Washington Post,* April 26, 1987, p. 4.
14. *Paganism in the Roman Empire* (New Haven: Yale University Press, 1982), p. 49.
15. *Ibid.*, p. 2.
16. *Pagans and Christians* (New York: Knopf, 1987).

NAME INDEX

Abel, 151f.
Abel, Reuben, 138
Abraham, 146,
Adler, Mortimer, 95
Anscombe, G. E. M., 170
Aquinas, Thomas, 26, 152
Aristotle, 137, 152,
Augustine, 28, 33, 133, 152

Barth, Karl, 133, 135
Bergan, Helen, 101
Berger, Peter, 170
Bloch, Ernst, 126
Bloom, Allan, 88, 169
Bultmann, Rudolf, 53, 133
Butterfield, Herbert, 24

Caesar, 148
Cain, 151f.
Calvin, John, 122, 157
Carlson, Allan, 34,
Castro, Fidel, 66
Childs, Brevard, 81
Cohn, Haim, 148
Colson, Charles, 119
Cooper, John O., 174
Costas, Orlando, 77

Dean, Thomas, 129
Derrida, Jacques, 135f.
Descartes, Rene, 132
Dobson, Ed, 74,
Dooyeweerd, Herman, 129, 158
Dulles, John Foster, 156
Dworkin, Ronald, 155

Eddy, Mary Baker, 53
Edwards, Jonathan, 55
Ellingsen, Mark, 73, 76ff., 168
Ellul, Jacques, 145
Engels, Friedrich, 155
Ezekiel, 48

Falwell, Jerry, 73ff.
Finney, Charles G., 55
Foakes-Jackson, F. A., 126
Fox, Robin Lane, 180
Frederick, Carl, 173
Frei, Hans, 81
Friedrich, Carl J., 159

Gandhi, Indira, 156
Geffré, Claude, 135
Gewirth, Alan, 155
Gould, Stephen J., 92,
Graham, Billy, 55, 74, 76, 103, 163, 166
Grotius, Hugo, 153f.
Gutierrez, Gustavo, 131

Hallowell, John H., 126, 159
Hammurabi, 150f.
Hart, H. L. A., 155
Hartshorne, Charles, 131
Hegel, Georg W. F., 92, 128, 130, 136
Heidegger, Martin, 135f.
Henkin, Louis, 148
Hesse, Hermann, 135
Hindson, Ed, 74
Hitler, Adolf, 16, 28, 33, 119, 130
Hook, Sidney, 140
Hume, David, 132
Hunter, J. D., 88, 139, 171f.
Huxley, Aldous, 135
Huxley, Julian, 135

Jeremiah, 48
Jesus, 16-21, 23, 29-32, 34f., 42ff., 46ff., 52, 54, 65-68, 70f., 96, 125, 131, 141, 148
Jones, Bob, 74
Josephus, 148

187

SUBJECT INDEX

Labor, 44
Law, 30, 44, 51, 69ff., 124, 145-
160, 167
Legislation, 29, 32, 34
Lesbianism, 26
Liberal arts, 91ff., 121
Liberal theology, 19, 66, 77, 145,
164f.
Liberation, 65, 126
Life, 18, 40f., 48, 51, 175
Literature, 44, 122, 139f., 169
Logos, 135-138
Love, 70f., 96, 125, 175
Lust, 40

Majority opinion, 33, 44
Marriage, 26, 174
Marxism, 18, 24, 65ff., 127, 130,
134, 156
Mass media, 19, 25f., 32, 34, 44,
54, 94, 111, 122f., 126, 132,
139, 174
Materialism, 15, 56, 68, 95, 128,
134
Matter, 127
Meaning, 58, 85, 127, 133, 138,
140
Methodology, 21
Mind, 27, 43, 59, 83, 89, 96f.,
135ff.
Mindset, 40, 43, 140, 142
Mission, 21, 39, 46ff.
Money, 45f., 99, 152, 173
Monogamy, 26f., 40, 69f., 119
Moral Majority, 25, 75
Murder, 30, 32, 69ff., 151

National Association of
Evangelicals, 76ff., 142, 168ff.
National Religious Broadcasters,
76
Naturalism, 24, 55, 88, 92, 126ff.,
132, 138ff., 155, 164, 176
Natural law, 28, 33, 145, 152ff.,
157ff.
Nature, 24, 35, 128, 131, 138,
177ff.
Nazis, 16, 154
Near Eastern religions, 145-147

Neighbor-love, 30f.
Neo-orthodoxy, 79
Nihilism, 138
Nuclear power, 29, 31

Obedience, 30, 54
Oppression, 56
Optimism, 165

Paganism, 15, 23, 25ff., 32, 55,
57-61, 83, 93, 124ff., 133ff.,
140, 164, 174, 176-182
Parents, 31, 34, 87
Peace, 24, 31
Pentecostalists, 87ff.
Perjury, 31
Phenomenology, 126
Philosophy, 15, 44, 67, 92ff., 112,
135ff., 139, 169
Piety, 17, 43
Pluralism, 16
Politics, 19f., 24, 32, 34f., 44,
54f., 66ff., 75, 92, 112, 121f.,
125f., 130, 172
Pornography, 26, 120
Poverty, 46, 55, 65ff., 150
Power, 56
Prayer, 46ff., 83, 172f.
Prison conditions, 55, 72
Process Philosophy, 53
Property, 152
Prosperity theology, 100ff.
Prostitutes, 42
Psychology, 121f., 141
Public welfare, 33
Purpose, 57, 125, 138

Reason, 16, 31, 33f., 59, 121,
135ff., 141
Reconciliation, 47
Reformation, 43, 82f., 96, 134,
157ff., 165
Refugees, 76, 175
Regeneration, 17, 21, 29, 126f.,
165, 167
Relativism, 27, 44, 115ff., 128,
169f.
Religion, 176ff., 180ff.
Religious freedom, 24f., 28, 47, 175